THE GALLERY GIRL

MIRROR BOOKS

© Louise Allen 2025

Names and locations have been changed throughout in order to protect the identities of individuals. This book contains graphic descriptions of rape, sexual assault and domestic abuse.

The rights of Louise Allen to be identified as the author of this book have been asserted, in accordance with the Copyright, Designs and Patents Act 1988.

All rights reserved. No part of this publication may be reproduced, stored in a retrieval system, or transmitted, in any form or by any means without the prior written permission of the publisher, nor be otherwise circulated in any form of binding or cover other than that in which it is published and without a similar condition being imposed on the subsequent purchaser.

1

Published in Great Britain and Ireland in 2025 by
Mirror Books, a Reach PLC business,
5 St Paul's Square, Liverpool, L3 9SJ.

www.mirrorbooks.co.uk
@TheMirrorBooks

Print ISBN 9781917439428
eBook ISBN 9781917439435

Design and production by Mirror Books.

Printed and bound in Great Britain by
CPI Group (UK) Ltd, Croydon, CR0 4YY

Cover image: Shutterstock
(Posed by model)

This book was printed using
FSC approved materials.

SLAVE GIRLS

THE GALLERY GIRL

Louise Allen
with Theresa McEvoy

MIRROR BOOKS

Foreword

Through my work with Spark Sisterhood, the charity I co-founded to help young girls leaving care, I hear many terrible stories about County Lines, the criminal gangs that groom and trap children and young people to sell drugs. I have learned a great deal about the forms of modern enslavement that girls are drawn into.

It isn't a new thing, but we are finally starting to hear a little more about it.

When I was a teenager, about 14 years old or so, a couple of school friends and I were recruited to move drugs from Oxford to London via the National Express coach service and the train.

The thing is, we were just kids. We didn't know what we were doing. We were a group of vulnerable girls who didn't even realise that we *were* vulnerable. We had not an ounce of experience between us that might enable us to realise that we were such easy targets. We were targets not just because of our age, but because of that needy vibe we gave out.

County Lines recruiters seek out that kind of neediness and vulnerability. It is a criminal cult. I use the word 'cult', though there is no religion, other than fast, extreme capitalism and the perverse exploitation of children – both sexually and emotionally. The reach of County Lines is huge and it's growing every day.

All our children are potential slaves for this cult.

County Lines has a hierarchical structure. At the bottom it has its minions, the youngers, then the elders above them who find ways to wield power. 'Elders' is an interesting word. In some contexts, particularly within religious or cultural settings, 'elder' denotes a specific role of leadership, guidance, or wisdom. So even some of the language within County Lines sounds like the language of a cult. The youngers are paid to go into prison, taking wages from their elders in order to keep the next layer of County Lines intact and untouchable, keeping the elders out of prison to carry on with business. Effectively, they do the time for their bosses.

But the elders are only part of the problem, and are also victims themselves. It's the ones that you can't see who are the real criminals, always hiding, sometimes in plain sight, in roles in the very authorities and organisations that are publicly funded to educate, train and employ people to protect our children. The elders who enjoy their titles and power often have no clue how manipulated they are by their bosses in the shadows. The ones who look like the most respectable people in the community. Those at the top of the tree sit side by side with some very important and influential people, and that is an uncomfortable truth.

'Cuckooing' is another term used in this book. It means

taking over the property of a vulnerable person. The property then becomes a base from which to supply drugs, known as a 'trap house'.

I have fostered girls who have been involved in County Lines and experienced debt bondage, cuckooing or life in a trap house. I also, through Spark Sisterhood, meet girls who are too terrified to speak about what's going on for them.

The Gallery Girl is inspired by one such story, though names and places have been changed to protect the innocent and, sadly, for legal reasons, some of the guilty. My books are an attempt to help expose some of those uncomfortable truths that we, as a society, seem so reluctant to confront.

As a reader of this story I hope you find a new awareness and greater understanding of just how big and close to all of us this criminal cult is.

In the end, it will come down to numbers. With more of us watching, observing and really seeing, the chances are that more of us will not be content to turn a blind eye to what is happening around us.

I also look forward to the day when we no longer judge the children involved as criminals, but as the victims they truly are.

1

Candace

'Candy-girl, come *on*!' Lorna snaps.

Candace struggles to drag the shopping trolley up the steps behind her. She hates the trolley. It's an old-lady trolley, really. Tatty and in need of a wipe over. They'd inherited it when they moved into the flat. It had been left in the broom cupboard, her mum said. Candace doesn't remember. She was only a toddler then, back when her father had left and they had to come here.

When the trolley is empty, on the way to the shops, the wheels don't pull properly and it tips up and bangs into her legs. When it's got stuff in it on the way home, it makes her arms ache and it's too heavy to easily get up the stairs.

Candace stands at the top of the concrete stairs to take a breath, facing the next block of red-brick flats. She hates this view, too. She turns and heaves the trolley up the last three steps, pulling with both hands until it's standing on the concourse.

Lorna holds onto the railings to help pull herself up

the steps and joins Candace and the trolley. 'Well done, Candy-girl.'

Candace hates it when her mum uses that name too. It's babyish.

A neighbour she recognises, from the flat along from theirs, walks toward them, vaping. He wears a woolly hat, even though it's quite warm today, and blows a plume of smoke over Candace's head. It smells funny. Kind of sweet.

'Fucking lifts,' he says.

It's true. The lifts are always breaking down.

'Yeah. Council don't give a shit,' Lorna mumbles in reply.

Actually, Candace doesn't mind so much about the lifts. She prefers the stairs, especially on the way down, but even when they're carrying shopping back up. The stairs trap the cooking smells from the flats around. Spices, herbs and burnt toast. The lift smells really bad. It smells of toilets. Whenever she gets in, she holds her nose closed, using her fingers like a synchronised swimmer's nose-clip.

She copied the move from an old lady who lives on the floor above and now she does it every time. Evelyn makes Candace laugh. If they are ever in the lift together, the old lady rolls her eyes to the ceiling of the lift, pinches her nose and says, 'Pooaww, stinks.'

Evelyn is quite a hard word for Candace to say and it comes out as 'Evening'. It makes Candace giggle if she can say 'Evening, Evening'. She sometimes says it even if they see her in the morning.

Candace hasn't seen the old lady for a few weeks, though.

'Haven't seen Evening for ages,' Candace says.

Her mum's eyes dart about. 'Yeah, I think she's – she's on holiday.'

Her mum would know, because she sometimes does Evelyn's hair. Lorna still works as a hairdresser, though not very often because of the medicine she takes that makes her sleep a lot. But she doesn't do her hairdressing in a salon anymore, like she once did. Now her mum just goes into people's homes, with her scissors, mostly in this block of flats. She still has her hairdressing certificate in a frame on the wall. It's from the college where Lorna met Reg, Candace's dad. Candace doesn't remember her dad, but sometimes her mum talks about him.

Lorna trained in hairdressing and Reg trained as a chef. Her mum says they were in love, but Candace doesn't believe it. If they were really in love, then why did he leave and go to Glasgow? She'd like to see her dad, but Scotland is a long way away and her mum says no. When she's big enough, she'll try to find him. He works in a smart restaurant, so he'll be easy to track down – if he hasn't gone back to Trinidad. Her mum says that Trinidad is even further away than Scotland. She tried to show Candace a map on her phone, but it was too small to see properly. Candace thinks she'd like to go to lots of different countries when she's older.

Maybe she'll find Grandad Brian, too, in Ireland. She liked Grandad Brian, but he moved back to Ireland when Grandma Fi died, to move in with 'that whore', whoever she is. Candace doesn't really remember Grandma Fi. Lorna says she drank herself into liver failure, whatever that might be. But everyone leaving them and moving a long way away means that it's just Candace and her mum. There's no one else because they're all too far away.

'Me and you against the world, kid,' Lorna sometimes says.

Her mum and dad were only 18 when Lorna found out she was having a baby. Candace wasn't born in a hospital, she was born at home. Lorna says it was a big surprise; she didn't know the baby was going to come so quickly. Candace is five now and her mum is 24. She looks older than that though. Not as old as Evelyn, not like an old-old lady, but still old, with papery skin like Evelyn, and purple bits around her eyes.

At the top of the steps, litter has been swept to the side of the balcony. Chewing gum patterns the floor like the liver spots on the back of Evelyn's hand. Perhaps the liver spots mean that Evelyn has liver failure too.

They reach the front door. It's painted bright blue, but there are curled-up bits like pencil sharpenings in places, and it's brown underneath them. Lots of the doors look the same along their balcony, but Candace would recognise theirs anywhere. It has a block of plywood in one of the six small, square windows. The others have glass in them.

Inside their flat is dark. Lorna likes to keep the curtains drawn most of the time, especially when she's sleepy. Candace spends a lot of time playing on her mum's phone when Lorna is sleepy.

Sometimes Lorna gets up, opens all the curtains and windows and cleans up – even the ashtrays. Candace prefers it when her mum is like that, like she's had new batteries put in. The flat smells nicer with the new-batteries version of her mum. Lorna smokes lots of cigarettes, a *lot* of cigarettes, and they are stinky. She gets them in big packets from a man in one of the flats who goes on holiday a lot. The man comes round and stays sometimes, when he isn't on holiday. Candace doesn't like him very much. They make loud noises when she's in bed trying to sleep. Sometimes it sounds as if her mum is in pain.

The old lady, Evelyn, always asks Candace if she's started school yet. It's her favourite question. Candace shakes her head whenever the question comes. She isn't quite sure what school is, but sees other kids being walked along the passage down the stairs and out into the big courtyard in the mornings. Mums with buggies and prams, sometimes dads holding their kid's hand as they rush away. They have smaller bags than the shopping trolley. It would be nice to have a smaller bag, but Candace doesn't know how to get one.

Her mum gets annoyed when Evelyn asks about school, and sometimes she makes mistakes. She thinks that Candace is only four. 'But tall for her age.'

Candace: The Gallery Girl

Candace is certain she is five, because there were five candles on her birthday cake. Her mum should remember that, but she has to make allowances because the sleeping medicine makes her forget things.

Today the tartan trolley is nearly full to the top. They've been to Lidl. They have bought lots of pasta and some sauces, a loaf of white bread, some milk, toilet roll and a big bag of different flavoured packets of crisps. Today they also have cakes, which is another extra. Candace asked if they could put them in the trolley and Lorna said, 'Oh, alright, go on then.' Candace was surprised. Usually her mum says no. After Lidl they went to Home Bargains and Poundstretcher to buy some colouring pens and a scrap book. And then to the petrol station. They don't have a car, but by the side of the petrol station, on the path, is where they always wait for the man.

Candace doesn't like this man, either. He is very thin, like her mum. Like a stick insect she saw on a nature programme. Everything about him is dirty. His black hoodie is dirty, and his baggy black tracksuit bottoms and his dirty old trainers. He is very, very tall, and around his eyes his skin is a muddy grey colour, like the water at the canal on a rainy day.

Candace doesn't know where he comes from; he always seems to just appear. Then Lorna gives him money. Candace has to pretend not to see. Her mum has told her that lots of times, so Candace holds the trolley and makes shapes with her foot in the mud by the path so it doesn't look as if she's watching them. That's where her mum gets the medicine from. It always comes in a little packet, but Candace isn't allowed to hold it.

When they get home, Candace helps unpack the trolley, puts the food in the fridge and cupboard, and takes the loo roll to the bathroom.

Lorna starts cooking pasta for their dinner. She has to do it straight away when they get in, because if she sits down or lies down, she forgets and then Candace has to eat bread instead of dinner. Her mum doesn't eat very much, but Candace is always hungry. Her mum prefers to sit at the little table, smoking a roll up and flicking the ash onto her plate. She puts the TV on. Candace already knows what she's going to say next.

'Mummy's going for her sleep now, baby.'

Candace checks on her after a while. The spoon and the lighter and the belt are by the bed, and her mum has her mouth open, doing the slow-breathing she does after taking her medicine.

Candace tiptoes in, takes Lorna's phone and returns to the sofa and TV. She has to stay awake to look after her mum when she has these kinds of sleeps.

II

Candace

In the morning, Candace can hear people walking past their flat, talking in very loud voices. She pulls the curtains back in the kitchen as far as they will go. They are dusty, dark-orange curtains, the same in every room. They didn't choose the curtains, they came with the flat, and the linings are stained and torn. The kitchen window, which looks out onto the balcony, is smeared with dirt and condensation. Candace rubs the glass. She needs to get a better view. Something is going on. It looks like men from the council and they are taking things away from Evelyn's flat upstairs. Why are they taking all of Evelyn's things away?

She wrestles with the kitchen window, trying to push open the latch. It's so sticky it feels like someone has glued the frame shut. She perseveres and is rewarded when it suddenly jerks open, letting in some air and allowing Candace to hear the voices of the caretaker and the council men.

It turns out the old lady on the next floor didn't go on holiday. She died.

Candace thinks she knows what that means. You go away to heaven, like Grandma Fi. She opens the window a little bit more so that she can hear more of what they're saying. First they take out the sofa and a big lamp. Then comes a stained mattress. She can see them taking it down the stairs at the end of the balcony. Next is an empty birdcage. Had there been a bird in it, Candace wonders. She wants to ask them if she can keep the birdcage. She liked the old lady a lot.

The caretaker is telling the council men in their bright yellow jackets that Evelyn lived in the flat for over 60 years, moving in some time after the war when the flats were newly built.

She must have been a very, very old lady, Candace thinks.

'She was in the WRAF during the 50s, after the war,' the caretaker tells them. 'Flying aeroplanes! Life was different back then,' he says, wistfully. 'Everyone knew each other and all the balconies were immaculate. The residents all swept outside their front doors, and cleaned the stairs, or at least didn't drop litter. And put plant pots on the balcony, some of 'em even grew runner beans and tomatoes. It was a different world. People had a bit of pride back then, and they shared what they had. Not like now.'

Candace tries to imagine the balcony filled with plants and things growing. It sounds nice.

'Her husband died years ago,' the caretaker says. 'Got a couple of daughters, somewhere in Essex, I think. But they never come and visit. Sad really, that this is all there is to show for a life.'

Lorna has woken up and comes to stand behind Candace in the kitchen. That's unusual, because mostly Candace has to try lots of times to wake her up. Today, when Candace turns around, she sees that her mum is crying.

'Don't cry, Mummy. She was very old.' But Candace feels sad, too.

'Close the window. It's cold.'

Candace wishes they could keep the window open. It smells much nicer with the window open. It smells of fresh air and escape. But she does as she's told and pulls it shut tight. 'Shall I make you your cup of coffee?'

Candace is used to making the coffee in the morning. She does it most days. She has some burn marks on her hands and arms from accidentally touching the boiling kettle, but they are all old. She has learnt how not to do that anymore. The sharp pain and sores have taught her to be more careful.

While the kettle is boiling, Candace pulls the long curtains back in the lounge. She has to climb onto the back of the sofa to reach and tug the curtains along their old, yellowing, plastic curtain rail. Sometimes the back of the sofa rocks. Candace doesn't like it when that happens. She sometimes holds on to the big glass windowpane to make sure she doesn't fall.

These windows always feel a bit wet on the inside.

You can draw pictures in the wet. Candace likes to draw animals. And sometimes the shape of a sun. That way she can pretend that the sun is shining in their home, even when the days are grey and dark.

In front of the sofa is a grubby glass table that has sharp metal corners. Candace has a few scars from those corners, too. The glass top is sticky with rings from glasses of squash and coffee, but Candace knows not to wipe it, because sometimes there is white powder on the glass and her mum gets cross if Candace touches it.

Most days Candace switches on the TV and watches *Good Morning Britain* by herself. Candace likes watching TV. Sometimes when she watches she sees glimpses of the worlds that other people have. Children with lots of nice clothes and toys and this amazing place called school where lots of children sit in rooms and smile and put their hands up. Today, Candace stares at the TV wondering how she could look like Susanna Reid, the presenter. They both have dark hair, but Susanna's is very shiny.

But today they can watch together, because her mum is already awake! Candace sits on the sofa, her legs poking off the end. 'Mum, come and watch!'

She wants to show her mum the dogs on TV. They are very funny. If there is one thing that Candace would love, it's a dog.

Eventually her mum staggers into the lounge, wearing an old, discoloured T-shirt that just about covers her knickers. Lorna sits down next to her on the old sofa and wipes her nose with the back of her hand, sniffing at the same time. She puts her arm around Candace and plays with her hair.

'Your hair is just like your dad's.'

Candace knows she has the same kind of hair her dad has. Her mum says this a lot.

'Your father has a lot to answer for.'

She's seen a picture of him. Her father's hair is brown and really curly, also not straight and shiny like Susanna Reid's. She wishes she didn't have her father's hair. Not just because it doesn't go straight, but because it reminds her mum of him, and that's sometimes another reason for her mum to get sad. Not today though.

'Luv, can you make Mummy some toast? Be an angel.'

Candace doesn't know where that picture went. She'd like to have a picture of her dad. She slides off the sofa, pleased to help, and heads back to the kitchen. She pulls a couple of slices of white bread from the limp plastic bag. It's sunny today and the bag has got warm through the window. She has a little step which she pulls out so she can reach the toaster. She takes out the margarine from the small fridge. They have run out of jam and she didn't remember to get it when they went shopping yesterday. She slides both pieces of toast onto a plate and walks it back to her mum.

'Is that coffee ready, baby?'

Candace has forgotten about the coffee. She goes back out again to make it. Her mum likes it black and it helps her mum to wake up.

'Pass my phone, luv.'

Lorna looks at her phone and puffs out her cheeks. She tuts. 'I've got a busy day and not enough time.'

Candace doesn't understand this. There seems to be lots and lots of time every day. Too much time. And her mum doesn't do very much in the daytime. But she's probably talking about having to meet the stick insect man again.

After several more cups of coffee and lots more television, Lorna gets dressed. It's time to drag the shopping trolley down the stairs again. Candace pretends that the trolley is a lazy dog and coaxes it along the balcony. She calls the trolley 'Bailey', because that was the name of the dog on the morning television programme. She coaxes it along as she bumps it down all the way to the bottom. She doesn't hate the trolley nearly so much now that it's a dog.

At the bottom of the stairs, near the bins, Candace sees the birdcage from Evelyn's flat. They must have forgotten to put it in the van.

'Can I keep it?'

Her mum shrugs. 'If you want. You have to carry it, though.'

Candace imagines a brightly-coloured parrot inside. She calls it 'Reg', after her dad. Now she has two pets. It isn't far to carry the cage with Reg and to pull Bailey along on his lead. Today they are only going to the small Co-op in the precinct.

'I 'aven't got it in me to walk all the way to Lidl,' her mum says.

They go through the door. Candace reminds Bailey and Reg to be good while they are inside. Everything is in a kind of line in this shop, so you can only go one way round. They make their journey around the shop. The glass cold cabinets are at the back. Candace looks at all the milkshakes. They look so yummy. She puts her hand out to the cool of the glass and imagines the taste of them in her mouth.

'Come on,' Lorna says. 'We only came in 'ere for bread and milk.'

There is a man standing next to them. He smiles at Candace. Candace turns back for a last look at all the milkshakes: thick creamy banana, strawberry, chocolate, vanilla.

'Which one is your favourite?' the man says.

Candace looks up at him. He has a sandy beard and is wearing a cream-coloured T-shirt and jeans. He looks very strong. He is standing like a superhero and has big muscles that make it seem as if his arms only just fit into the T-shirt. He smiles and gives her an encouraging nod.

Candace puts her index finger onto her chin, frowns and makes a 'hmm' noise.

'Chocolate,' she says, after a moment.

The man gives a little laugh. 'Good choice. It's mine too.'

Lorna is not far away, over by the bakery section. She has a packet of crumpets in her hand and Candace is excited for a moment, but then her mum puts them back on the shelf.

Candace skips toward the counter where her mum is taking milk and beans out of the basket and putting them onto the counter.

'Maybe we should get a scratchcard,' Lorna says. 'Am I feeling lucky today?' But just like with the crumpets, she changes her mind. She passes the items down to Candace to put in the trolley.

Candace notices that the man with the beard has put a bottle of his favourite chocolate milkshake on the counter and pays for it along with tobacco and Rizlas. He walks behind Lorna and Candace, and just as they step outside he hands the milkshake to Candace.

'Enjoy,' he says with a smile and walks away.

Candace is so excited. It's definitely *her* lucky day. 'Mummy, look. Chocolate shake.'

Her mum stares after the man.

When they get home, while Candace puts the shopping away, Lorna has a shower, washes her hair and puts some make-up on her face. She takes a lot of time doing this. She puts on a clean T-shirt and some tight jeans.

'I look so fat,' she moans, when she looks in the mirror.

Candace doesn't think she looks fat. Her mum looks skinny and bony.

Then Lorna starts cleaning. She wipes down the sticky coffee table, scrubbing really hard to get all of the marks off.

Candace sits down on the sofa. She's tired from the trip to the shops, and a little bit confused by her mum's sudden burst of activity. She wonders what has caused it. Maybe it will mean a trip to the park to feed the ducks, or something else to do, something that isn't dragging the tartan trolley to the shops. They used to go to the park, when Candace was still in a buggy. She remembers the ducks.

It's as if her mum is a mindreader, or her wishes really can come true, because all of a sudden Lorna says, 'Let's go out for a walk this afternoon.'

Candace feels so proud of her mummy today.

It's a long walk to the park, but Lorna is jolly and smiley all the way, like the other mummies. She holds Candace's hand when they are in the park, and when they are near the pond, she lifts her hand up and says 'Weeee'.

Because they are walking so close together, they bump into each other when their steps don't match up and it makes Candace giggle. Her mum looks around, as if she is looking for someone. Candace hopes it's not the stick-insect man. For once they didn't go home via the garage after the shops. Lorna's heart sinks, maybe she is meeting him here instead.

The pond has a big fence around it, and behind the fence the pond is full of ducks. They haven't brought any bread with them, but a lady in a blue coat gives her some of hers. The ducks come rushing up to eat the bread, gobbling it all up.

They stay for a while, but however much her mum looks into the middle distance, whoever she is looking for doesn't appear. Suddenly Lorna suggests that they go to the sweet shop. 'How about some candy for my Candy-girl?' It really is her lucky day!

Candace has never been in the sweet shop before, although it isn't much further than the park. Inside there is a wall of glass jars with screw lids on different shelves. There is an old man behind the counter who has nice eyes.

There are so many sweets that she feels overwhelmed and can't make a decision about which ones she wants.

This makes her mum cross and Candace doesn't want Lorna to get angry. She wants to keep the perfect, smiley mum. The old man smiles.

'Why don't you try out a few, all in one bag? Do you trust me to choose for you?'

Candace nods solemnly, as he points out his different recommendations. He makes Candace feel special and very grown-up.

Candace leaves the beautiful sweet shop clutching a paper bag, now with the agonising pleasure of thinking about which of the selection to eat first.

Apart from finding out that Evelyn was dead, this really is the best day ever.

III

Candace

On the walk home, Lorna's buoyant mood seems to have disappeared as quickly as it arrived. Perhaps it's because Candace took so long choosing in the sweet shop. They call into the little newsagents near the flats. As well as newspapers, it is stocked with wall-to-wall vapes, alcohol and a table where people return packages for Amazon. Lorna picks up a large, plastic bottle of cheap cider.

When they get back up to the flat, Candace makes herself a sandwich of bread and butter – still no jam – and sits on the sofa to eat it. Her mum is now in a bad mood. Candace must have done something wrong. Her mummy can be very moody, and Candace usually puts it down to something she has done to upset her.

'Sorry, Mummy,' she says. She regrets having the sweets and enjoying the ducks. She feels very lonely. She prefers the medicine to the big cider bottle; when her mum drinks from the apple bottle she can become very shouty.

Her mum sits in the chair away from Candace, watching the TV and drinking the cider like it's water. Candace feels very worried. She slips down from the sofa and begins tidying up the flat as best she can. When she returns, Lorna is still sitting in the chair, her head dropped down. Her breath is much louder, more like snoring. In her right hand is half a roll-up. It has gone out. Candace places it carefully in the ashtray so that it doesn't drop while her mum is sleeping.

In the morning, when Candace comes into the sitting room and climbs up on the back of the sofa, unknowingly risking her life to open the curtains, her mum isn't there. She must have woken up in the night and gone to bed. Candace makes a cup of tea with two sugars and takes it to the bedroom. Lorna lifts herself onto the two pillows that Candace moves behind her. Her mum breathes out and the stench of tobacco and cheap cider is strong. So strong that Candace flinches away, hoping that her mother doesn't see.

She returns to the dreary lounge and turns on the TV, settling herself down on the seat cushion with her legs sticking forwards off it. Eventually Lorna stumbles in, swearing and moaning. Lorna goes to the kitchen to put the kettle on for a cup of coffee and Candace jumps up to help. Candace is filling up the kettle when a shadow crosses the window. She looks up. It's a man passing by. The same man who gave her the chocolate milkshake yesterday.

'He must know someone in the flats, or maybe he's

moved in to one of them,' Lorna murmurs. She suddenly darts from the room.

'Come on, baby-girl, let's go for a walk and see the birds in the trees,' her mum calls from the bathroom.

Candace is excited by the prospect of another day out. She hears the sound of the shower going on again. Her mum never usually showers two days in a row.

When Lorna opens the door to let the steam out afterwards, Candace can watch her mother getting ready. She brushes her hair, then applies some make-up. She tries to do it with one hand at first, but then has to put her roll-up down alongside the other, shorter fag ends that are sitting in in the chipped, flower-patterned saucer in the bathroom.

Lorna pinches her cheeks, then slaps them and says out loud, 'Come on, gal, sort yourself out. He's not gonna wanna shag a corpse.'

The slap brings a little colour to her cheeks. Lorna peers at her reflection in the mirror once more and smiles. 'Go get it!'

Candace doesn't really understand what her mum is talking about, but is just happy to see her look better and sound cheerier. She soaks up each drop of joy her mum delivers, a smile, the touch of her hand. Starved of affection, she will take it wherever she can, catch it and hold onto it.

Her mum makes them both some toast and puts on the radio. The DJ announces the next track: 'Diamonds' by

Rihanna. Her mum shakes out her arms. 'I love this one!' she says.

As soon as it begins, Lorna sings along with every word and dances her way round the kitchen. Candace looks on, delighted.

After they've finished their toast and butter, Lorna leaves the plates on the little table. When Candace reaches out to tidy up, Lorna waves her away.

'Leave it, baby, let's get outside.'

The trolley is not in action today; it stands by the door.

'No walk for you today, Bailey,' Candace says on their way out.

It's a nice, fair-weather day, not too hot or cold. The light is crisp and clear and the sky is the same blue as Candace's paintbox.

They walk along the balcony to the stairs. They don't bother with the lift. They do one level, turn the corner and walk straight into milkshake man.

He is bounding up the steps, two at a time, with a tin of paint and a paintbrush. He looks up and sees Candace and Lorna.

'Hey, chocolate milkshake girl!' he says.

Candace smiles and Lorna seems keen to stop and chat. She never usually wants to talk to people.

'Oh, hello. I just wanted to say thank you for buying the milkshake for Candy. I didn't have a chance to say thank you yesterday.'

'Candy? Cool name.'

Candace blushes. She's never thought about the name 'Candace' much before. It's just her name. But she decides that as long as it isn't 'Candy-girl', perhaps she quite likes 'Candy'.

'You guys live here, then?'

Candace is straight in with the enthusiasm of her nearly six years. 'Yes, we live there!' She points along the balcony to their front door.

The man nods. 'Well, I live up there,' he says, pointing to Evelyn's old flat, above them on the next floor. 'Just moved in.'

Although it was Candace who spoke, he's looking at Lorna as he says it.

Lorna is looking back at him, right in the eye. She must really like him, Candace thinks, because she usually looks away from people and tries to get away from them as quickly as she can.

'On your own?' Lorna says.

'Just me at the moment, but when I've finished decorating, a friend of mine's going to move in.'

'Your girlfriend?' Candace asks, with the directness that only a five-year-old can get away with.

'No. Just a friend.' He holds up the tin of paint. 'I just got this off the caretaker. The walls need freshening up with a lick of paint.'

Candace doesn't know what to say next, and neither, it seems, does her mum. There is an awkward pause as they all look at each other for a moment.

'I like painting,' Candace says.

'Well, perhaps you can come and help me,' the man says.

'Not that sort of painting, Candy. You like painting in your colouring book.'

Candace is cross that her mum has said that. Painting is painting.

'I'm Billy, by the way,' the man says.

Candace, remembering that it is polite to do introductions, says, 'My mummy's name is Lorna.'

The man smiles at Candace again. 'And what are you two up to today? You look as if you're off out.'

Candace announces that they are going to see the birds in the tree. 'I'm very excited.'

Billy does the thing of looking at Lorna again, while answering Candace at the same time. 'Yeah? Wow, that's awesome. You have an amazing day, and I look forward to hearing all about those birds, Candy.'

They say goodbye.

'See you around,' Lorna says.

'I hope so,' Billy says, and he stares at Candace's mum again.

Candace holds her mum's hand as they skip down the remaining flight of stairs, chattering away. 'Billy's nice,' she giggles.

'Sshhh. He'll hear you!' Lorna says.

'So? I'm sad that Evening's gone, but I'm glad Billy and his friend will be living in her flat.' Candace is wondering if her future might hold a few more milkshakes with Billy around.

'So am I.'

Yes. Her mum definitely likes Billy. Candace has seen that look in her eyes before.

'Hmmm.' Lorna is chewing her bottom lip, which means she's thoughtful.

At the bottom of the stairs, they go past another neighbour, the nosey lady at number 10 who has posh white net curtains. She points up towards Billy on the next balcony, where he's just heading into Evelyn's old flat.

'You wanna watch that one,' she says. 'Just out of prison. They've turned Evelyn's place into a halfway house for ex-offenders.'

IV

Billy

Lorna is a smackhead. He's met enough of them. Knows how desperate they are – and what they'll do. The fact that she has a kid makes it even better. Oh yes, he's come across plenty of Lornas. He could feel her eyes on him as he walked back to the flat. She would have been eyeing up his muscles. His shoulders are broad and his arms are strong. He's spent the last few months working on his physique – there was nothing much else to do – and knows that he looks good. A smackhead like Lorna would be desperate for a man like him to take care of her. But – softly, softly, catchee monkey.

Time to work on the flat first, get it into a nice shape before Joey arrives. There are two bedrooms and a decent-sized lounge. It feels like a mansion after a prison cell. The kitchen and bathroom are old-fashioned, but will be clean enough once Billy has finished with the bleach. Nobody could accuse him of not being house-proud. Perhaps it stems from his Irish traveller family roots. As a young kid he lived in a caravan and grew up in very different circumstances to his peers. Billy's family were tough, sometimes cruel, and he has always understood that to be a way of life. When his father shot another man on the traveller site, Billy was taken into care. His first few foster placements broke down quickly and he ended up ricocheting around different children's homes. With his possessions in bin liners and never feeling like he could call anywhere home, Billy is fastidious about keeping his place nice.

Growing up in care made him an easy target and he was recruited into County Lines at the age of eight, nearly 20 years ago now. Like so many recruits, he's done time on minimal sentences for the elders in the gang, on a wage to take the rap. Although he's been convicted on multiple occasions, boarding off and on at Her Majesty's pleasure since he was a teenager, he never stays in prison for long. Being well-connected includes having a good lawyer as well as people on the inside in high places. But also, Billy likes to think, because he is the man who takes care of things. And being that sort of man gets you a reduced sentence. You're needed on the outside.

These days he's lost most of his Irish accent. After his first custodial sentence in a young offenders' centre, he realised that Irish lads get a rough time. These days, Billy is hardcore. You don't mess with him and get away with it. Even the Albanians are scared of him. Billy comes from a long line of scary men – and women. Fear is his modus operandi.

Although Billy introduced himself to Lorna and Candy by his first name, he mostly goes by 'Bananas'. Everyone on the inside has a nickname and although Billy's stretches inside are short, he has still ended up spending more time in prison than out of it. The upside of this consistency is that he is well-known and well-connected. 'Bananas' has stuck because it beautifully telegraphs how violent and disconcerting he is capable of being.

The last stretch was for attempted murder and arson. That's where he met Joey Samaroo. They shared a cell. Joey was what Billy liked to call a 'gentler' sort of criminal, in there for drug dealing rather than anything violent. Joey, like so many in prison, started his criminal career at school when he was recruited in the toilets by taking a vape from an older boy. Before he knew it, he was a mule taking drugs across the country, jumping trains for the Albanians. He just got caught in the wrong place at the wrong time. Billy looked after Joey a bit inside and still feels protective over the younger man. Yes, he's looking forward to seeing Joey again. He's got big plans for young Joey Samaroo.

Although Billy generally made a point of cultivating associates rather than friends, strangely, he and Joey just clicked. Billy had enjoyed Joey's quiet but sharp humour and, in return, Billy had made sure that no one touched Joey, who would otherwise have been an easy target. Joey's release date is still a few days away, which has given Billy time to move into the flat with the idea of seeking out a potential trap house nearby and some new mules. And what do you know? A little opportunity seemed to have just presented itself to him before he'd even needed to go looking for it. All his wishes for business nestling in the flat below him. Bingo!

Billy whistles as he finishes a second coat of gloss on the window frames, almost unable to believe his luck. He starts unpacking some of his things onto the new shelves he's put up in the sitting room. Billy would like to stay on the outside now that he's got this place and some prospects on the horizon. Big prospects, too. Growing up in caravans and care, with nothing to his name that wouldn't fit inside a single bin liner, he has inherited a taste for knick-knacks. An ornament makes a place look homely, Billy feels. Most of Billy's things have been acquired through burglaries he's committed. When he sees something that takes his fancy, he helps himself. This Lorna might just be that next thing. Not that he fancies her, as such, but she is a means to an end. She and that cutesy little daughter of hers. What was her name? Candy?

This would be better than taking candy from a baby, this would be taking Candy from a smackhead.

Over the next few days he makes a point of bumping into the junkie and the kid. He smiles every time. The stupid bitch laps it up. More than laps it up. She actually looks like she's making an effort with her appearance. Make-up, doing her hair and that.

Billy watches their routine carefully. If you can call it a

routine. He starts to notice what time of day she and the kid leave the flat, the kid dragging that ridiculous tartan trolley behind her. He works out that they tend to be out for about an hour. He finds a few jobs that need doing outside his own flat and times them so that he can be in position to call down a greeting from above when they open their front door.

There's another reason to look forward to Joey's release date. He'll fit nicely into the plan. Because this time, he's thinking big.

Billy makes sure there's plenty of lager and a bit of coke and a spliff ready for Joey. They celebrate his release with a quiet night in, listening to music.

In the morning, Billy makes a fry-up, filling the flat with the smell of bacon, eggs and toast. He hasn't got a table yet, so the two men sit on the sofa, tucking into their breakfast. Billy introduces the topic close to his heart.

'There's a twat downstairs, directly below us called–, shit, I can't remember. Anyway, she's a smackhead. Needy bitch, I reckon. Worth a fuck but totally off 'er 'ead.'

Joey nods and smiles. 'That's handy, mate. You done her yet, then?'

'Nah, not yet. But I will,' Billy says.

Joey laughs.

Billy continues, 'She's white, right, but she's got this daughter who looks like you.'

Joey's grandad was part of the Windrush generation

who left the Caribbean to find better lives in England. Joey's mum married a white man she met at a Ska gig in Camden Town. Billy heard the whole fuckin' story when they were inside.

'I mean you could *be* her fuckin' dad!'

'Not guilty, mate,' Joey says, holding his hands in the air.

Billy sniggers. 'Nah, I meant she's mixed race, ya know. Same skin as you. Anyways, I want her out to work. We can walk her straight past the CCTV without any suspicion whatsoever.'

Billy knows exactly what to do to make this happen. He has a tried and tested formula that works every time, and it's a plan that they've already discussed in prison: how to get women to do what they want. It's straightforward because, as far as Billy is concerned, women are so stupid they believe any old bullshit. Best to find one that has been raped and abused. A violent or pervy dad or stepdad in the background is the best bet. Find one like that and they're up for anything – and bloody thankful, too. Women take any shit. Flattery, especially for the mingers, is golden. They're so grateful for it, they lap it up. Then they feel obligated to do whatever you want them to just to keep it coming.

'Ain't she at school?' Joey asks.

Billy laughs. 'Fuckin' twats like her don't even remember to take their kids to school. They're easy meat, mate. Almost too fuckin' easy. I've hardly put any effort into hooking her in.'

Joey smiles and rubs his hands together. 'Back in business!'

Joey is fully briefed on his role: he has to create a relationship with Candy, get her to trust him so that he can be seen out with her with no suspicion. It'll help that they look racially similar. Little kids make the best mules, because nobody thinks that they are anything but innocence personified.

Billy clears the plates, then sprays the inside of his mouth with peppermint spray before he manoeuvres himself into position, working on the gutter that goes down from his flat to the balcony below – right alongside the smackhead's place. When she opens the door with the kid and the trolley, there's Billy in a loose cotton shirt, conveniently falling open enough so that some of his six-pack is on display.

'That's it, Joey, just to the left,' Billy calls up to his partner. He smiles at the girl and then at the kid. 'Hello, sunshine.'

'Hello, Billy,' Candy says. 'This is my dog, Bailey.'

Billy can't see a dog, but nods along anyway and turns his attention to the kid's mum. 'So, I was wonderin'. D'ya fancy coming out for a drink?' He still can't actually remember what she said her name was, so he'll need to find a way to rediscover that without making it obvious that he's already forgotten.

The silly cow simpers and blushes as if she's a teenager. 'Yeah, alright.'

Billy smiles. 'Right answer!'

The smackhead lowers her head like a submissive pet.

'Are you around tonight, by any chance?' he asks her.

She shifts from foot to foot. 'Well, yeah, but I'd have to find a sitter for Candy.'

'I might be able to help you out there. See, my flatmate, Joey, up there, loves kids. He can come down and keep an eye on Candy for ya. Eh, Candy?'

Candy shrugs, unsure.

'Yeah, sure. What time?'

Christ. Even this bit's easy. The bitch doesn't give a toss about safeguarding her kid.

Billy stares into her eyes. 'Seven. I'll knock on ya door and Joey'll look after Candy. Yeah, Candy? You can play with Joey. He's just a big kid.'

Candy nods.

Amazing what one little milkshake can do.

'She'll be fine,' Billy winks. 'I'll see you at seven o'clock, then.'

Billy tracks down the caretaker and manages to get him to reveal Lorna's name. Then, as they're walking down the concrete stairs to her flat below, Billy reminds Joey that there should be, 'no kiddy fiddling!'

'Fuck off, mate, I'm not into that shit!'

Billy shrugs and knocks on the door. Joey stands behind him. Music is playing loudly inside the flat. Beyonce. The last lyric before it goes off is, *if you like it, then you shoulda put a ring on it.*

Billy raises his eyes to heaven and then the door opens.

As if a man like him would actually put a ring on the finger of a scumbag like Lorna.

'Lorna, Lorna, Lorna! You look bloody gorgeous!' he says. The repetition of her name is as much for his own benefit as it is for hers.

Because she looks far from gorgeous. Her ribs show through pale skin beneath her white crop top, and her hip bones are protruding noticeably through her skinny jeans. Her hair is tied up on the top of her head like a pineapple. A style that went out years ago, if it was ever truly in. But he can see the dark shape of a nipple in a little push-up bra behind the thin material of the crop top and he concentrates on that.

'I'm a lucky man being seen out with such a hottie,' he continues, staring at her as if she's a museum exhibit that he has a passionate interest in.

'Let's go then. Bye, Candy!' Lorna grabs her bag and the two of them leave through the front door.

Billy places his hand on her knobbly back. He is going to get her very drunk. Who knows, he might even enjoy himself. Mix a bit of business and pleasure.

V

Joey

The flat is cleaner and tidier than Joey expected, though there are stale smells of roll-ups and damp towels in the air, creating an unpleasant fug, in spite of the open window and the cloying perfume that seems to have been sprayed everywhere.

'We tidied up,' Candace says, noticing him looking around. 'Well, I did. When Mum was getting ready.' She pauses. 'I've got my toys out.'

He looks down to where she is pointing. A line of broken and tired toys are lined up against the skirting.

She seemed excited to have someone to play with, so he asks if she has many friends.

'No, we don't have friends round. Specially not for me.'

Jesus. She thinks he's her friend. Joey tries to muster some enthusiasm. He suspects this will be a long night.

'Well, little lady. What shall we do?'

Candy smiles up at him, with her trusting eyes. 'Can we play Rock-Paper-Scissors?'

Joey is momentarily thrown by this request. In spite of

the pitiful collection of toys, he expected her to suggest gaming, because isn't that what all kids do? With a sigh, he sits down opposite her, amused by the way her little hands fly out from behind her back to the space in front, like blades.

It doesn't take long before he's captivated by her laughter. She giggles every time she wins, delighted to be beating him. Joey doesn't mean to let her win; he finds that he's just too slow for her. There's only so many rounds of Rock-Paper-Scissors you can play, so after he has been well and truly trounced he suggests a game of Simon Says. He knows what his instructions from Billy are, but after the dull walls of his prison cell this cute kid is a breath of fresh air, and Joey realises that he's enjoying himself more than he has done for a long time.

He soon realises that Simon Says isn't the best suggestion for a game between two people, but they adapt the rules and take it in turns to put their fingers on their noses, hands on their heads and tummies and all of them at the same time until Joey topples over onto the floor, done in.

It's 9.30pm. More than two hours have passed by in a flash. But Candace is looking very sleepy and rubs her eyes.

'Have you had something to eat?' he asks.

Candace nods. 'We went to the chip shop because Mum said it was a special occasion.'

'Is it your bedtime?' Joey asks. He could do with a rest himself.

Candace: The Gallery Girl

By way of answer, Candace yawns, and it seems to take up her whole face, like a lion's roar. She stands up from the sofa, stares for a moment and then heads off, presumably to her bedroom.

Joey gives her a few minutes to get herself ready for bed. He's not quite sure what he should do for her; Lorna wasn't exactly forthcoming with instructions. A few minutes later, when he goes to check on her, she's fast asleep, holding onto a shabby old teddy. Joey looks around her room. He compares it to his own childhood bedroom which had a shelf of Transformer toys, a big Pokemon poster and a blue duvet set that was *Top Gear* inspired. The head of 'the Stig' from the show was on the pillow and his body on the cover. Joey loved that duvet set, and he loved his room. It was a far cry from this. Candace is nestled into a bed in the corner, surrounded by adult stuff, and an adult with hoarding tendencies at that. There are only a handful of toys and nowhere to play. Poor kid.

He goes into the lounge and puts on the TV. Someone is in the chair answering questions on *Who Wants to be a Millionaire?*. He doesn't really pay attention, content instead to scroll through his phone. After a while, he thinks he'll go and make himself a drink.

He looks around for a moment at the state of the kitchen and reaches for the fridge door. Inside is a nearly empty tub of Flora, some milk and a plastic bag with half a loaf or so of sliced bread. The sight depresses him, especially when he thinks of all the food stacked up on the shelves inside Billy's fridge. He shakes his head and again thinks, poor kid. Candace doesn't know that her mum is a junkie. How would she? To her all this is normal, it's just how they live.

He wonders about Candace's father. Who he is. Where he is.

Joey is the third generation of his family here. His grandfather came over in 1948 to help 'rebuild Britain' after the war. But he wasn't quite welcomed with the open arms he'd expected and worked the buses until he died.

His grandmother was a cleaner. Joey's mum married a white man. His family were nice enough, but out of their depth with a black daughter-in-law. His white grandparents came from quite a small village in Hampshire. His parents' marriage broke down when Joey was small. His dad remarried a woman who he knew at school. They went on to have three daughters and had no time for mixed-race Joey. He felt it keenly. He wonders if Candace feels that, yet. She will, in time.

His mum was left to struggle alone. She had her career as a nurse, but it didn't pay well. That's why, in part, he first got involved in County Lines. To help her out and earn a little bit of extra money. How misguided it was, he knows now. It soon escalated to being terrified that his mum would be raped and killed by the elders in the gang if he didn't do exactly what was asked of him. And now he barely sees her. When he 'turned bad' as a teenager, his mum couldn't cope. These days they exchange the odd text message. Funny how life turns out. His mum moved to Belgium three or so years ago to be near her sister, Joey's auntie, and their family, heartbroken and embarrassed when Joey ended up inside.

Being in prison was the worst experience of his life. It was overcrowded and violent, and it was near-on impossible to escape a beating. Thank God for Billy, who looked after him in those darkest moments. Because Joey became aware, very early on, that he wasn't cut out for prison life. Systems were complicated. It was hard trying to navigate the good screw from the gang screws.

Lorna probably has a similarly bleak story. You don't become a junkie because life's handed its riches to you on a plate. So she's another kid like him caught up in the middle of it all.

But he has a job to do. There's no point going soft. He's a criminal. That's the path he's found himself on. He has a job to do, he tells himself again, focusing his concerns on the logistical things: will Candace be paid for the work she is about to do? Will Lorna be paid for allowing her daughter to do it? He doubts it, but it's clear from looking around this flat that Lorna's struggling. Of course she is. Why else would Billy target her?

It's another couple of hours before Lorna and Billy return, flying through the door, three sheets to the wind, laughing, giggling and all over each other.

'Is she alright?' Lorna slurs. 'Is my li'l girl alright?'

'She's fine,' Joey reassures her. 'We played some games. She went to bed a while back and she's fast asleep now.'

Joey sees Billy's arm is draped over Lorna's shoulder, the loose hand fondling her breast.

Billy winks at Joey. 'Go on, then, fuck off and leave us to it. See yous laters.'

Joey nods and smiles. 'Have fun.' He closes the door gently behind him as he leaves.

Lorna might be a junkie, but that kid's done nothing wrong. He feels a little bit bad for what's about to happen, then shakes his head again as he trudges back up the concrete steps to their flat. Not his business.

He's lying on his bed, with his arms behind his head, listening to music when he hears Billy come in a while later.

Billy walks straight into Joey's room without knocking. He tugs on his belt and lifts his fingers to his face to smell them. He laughs and it turns into a leer. 'I needed that more than I realised. And the beauty of it is, I've got myself some cunt whenever I want it.'

Joey nods without saying anything, hoping that Billy will get the hint and disappear. He doesn't like this kind of talk.

He wishes the world wasn't the way it is. He doesn't want to get that little girl involved in anything. He wishes there was a way out of this whole situation. But there's no point.

There never is.

VI

Joey

In the morning Joey wakes to the sound of Billy banging about in the kitchen. The smell of coffee mixes with the smell of his roll-up.

Joey heads out to join Billy, where he has pulled a kitchen chair onto the balcony to sit in the sun.

Billy grunts, engrossed in sending a text message. He looks up when Joey sits down.

'That was the boss. Wanting to know if everything's in place. I've told him we're nearly in but we need a few more days. So we've got to crack on.'

Joey nods. They both have their roles to play. Billy will carry on working on Lorna, while Joey befriends Candace and works towards taking Candace off Lorna's hands.

'Make out you're doing her a favour. Daft bitch won't be any the wiser.' Billy rubs his hands together. 'It's a good day for business, I reckon we can get in that flat by tomorrow, set up the kitchen and get little Candy to work.'

The cuckoo operation of Lorna and Candace's flat is swift. It takes just a day and a half before there are three men working in the kitchen, cooking crack, measuring cocaine, packaging up ketamine and other drugs. This lot have been dispatched by the regional leaders who send them to new trap houses in groups of three. An apprentice will join them soon, learning the craft so that they can be part of the team dispatched to the next trap house.

Lorna is kept nice and quiet with the promise of as much free gear as she wants.

Joey is adamant that Candace shouldn't be allowed in her kitchen while all this is going on. He takes her to the park and gives her meal deals or orders pizza. She can eat it in the lounge, or her bedroom, but the kitchen is out of bounds. By the end of the week Lorna is happily shooting up every day. Candace has effectively lost her mum but gained a protector in Joey.

'How's the kid with you?' Billy asks.

'Sweet, yeah. She's good.'

Billy also spends some time with Candace and Joey. They go back to the park and buy ice creams. It's almost too easy. No one gives them a second glance. Candace and Joey safely look like they could be related. Daughter and father at best, or daughter and uncle.

'And I'm just a friend tagging along for good measure,' Billy chuckles.

Candace is relaxed in their company; the constant promise of milkshakes, ice creams, pizzas and meal-deals is good currency for bonding with a lonely, hungry five-year-old.

They head for the swings. Joey pushes Candace while Billy looks on, making the appropriate 'good girl' comments and 'weeeeee' sounds.

Candace seems happy. 'I didn't have any dad and now I've got two,' she says.

Joey has to look away when she says that.

On Monday, the plan proper for Candace kicks into action.

Billy goes into Lorna's room in the morning, when she's only half awake. Joey waits in the hall.

'Babes, look, I'm taking Candy to school.'

'That's great. She really needs to go to school,' Lorna slurs. Perhaps she's too out of it to remember that her daughter hasn't ever been to school. Perhaps on some subconscious level she knows that Candace should already be at school and feels grateful that someone else might be sorting that out for her. Maybe she just feels relieved that she doesn't have to think about her daughter all day. It's clever work by Billy and so easy.

'Yep, it's the right thing for her. You leave it with me, darlin'.'

Joey gathers up the purchases he has made under Billy's instruction. A generic, pale-pink girls' rucksack from Poundland. A plain cream baseball cap, with no brand name or distinguishing features.

'She's got to be able to just disappear into the crowds,' Billy had said.

The rucksack has been loaded up with kush – a kind of

cannabis – plus wraps of cocaine and ketamine. At the top of the inside of the rucksack, covering the drugs, is a meal deal offer and some sweets. Candace's eyes light up with glee when she sees them.

'You're just going on a little bus trip into town with Billy,' Joey explains, as he puts the rucksack on Candace's back and tightens the straps. Billy has planned some upmarket business today. He has a load of clients in the West End. The bus is slower, but safer than the tube. The transport police are sharp and pose the biggest threat to operations. Billy's gang don't worry too much about the ordinary pigs, but transport police are different. On the underground there are witnesses, CCTV, ticketing staff to dodge. No, the buses are a much better bet when they can be used.

Joey feels sick about plunging Candace into this world, but he knows he has no choice. The best he can do is exist within the system and try to protect Candace as much as he can. Minimise the damage.

'Can I bring Bailey?'

Joey is confused for a moment. 'Who's Bailey?'

Candace points at the trolley. What the hell does she want with that? Aside from the fact that it's intended for someone eight decades older than the kid, it's very distinctive. She'll stand out like a sore thumb with that.

'Er, no. Not today. It'll be tricky on the escalators. But you don't need it. You've got your nice new rucksack.'

Billy comes back out into the hall. 'Ello, darling, you

ready for a nice outing, then? How do you like your special new rucksack?'

Candace smiles and nods.

Joey can see that Billy was right. A kid who has known nothing but chaos and poverty in her short life will be so easy to control with a few treats here and there.

Billy pulls the cap down firmly on her head. 'We don't want you getting sunburn, do we, now?'

Candace shakes her head, clearly enjoying all the attention.

She runs in to her mum.

'Bye, Mummy. See you soon.' She kisses her mum on the cheek, but Lorna barely stirs in response.

'Good girl,' Billy says. 'You'll see Mummy later, yeah.'

'Have a good day, Candy,' Joey says.

'Aren't you coming, too?' Candy's face drops.

'Not today, I've got other work to do.'

He watches as Billy holds Candace's hand while they walk down the stairs. Billy's looking at his phone, probably checking delivery details.

Candace tries to swing her arm with him, Billy seems to find this irritating and breaks off.

'Yeah, Cands, that's fun and all, but let's go to the shop and get you a comic, shall we?'

Again, Joey wishes he could do something to stop this happening. At the very least, it should be him taking Candace. He'd at least swing her arm while they walked.

He shakes his head and goes back inside.

VII

Billy

Billy's happy. This isn't the first time he's done this, but it's been one of the quickest and most straightforward of operations. The modus operandi is well-practised and it works. His gang targets single mothers, preferably those with just one child. Normally they watch schools and follow mums and kids home, checking to see if there's a bloke about and, if not, Billy moves in on them. Billy's job is to go in first and groom the mother. Women love him and he can be very charming. He knows which women to go for. He always fucks them and then he gets them onto drugs – if they're not on them already. If they are, he increases their dose. His bosses will be pleased he's managed to act so quickly this time.

The kid has his arm and is trying to swing it, which Billy is already finding irritating, but manages to hold himself back from telling her off. He's trying to sort out the deals on his phone. He doesn't want anyone's attention. He doesn't want to do anything that might invite people to take a second look at them. So he has a quiet word so that she shuts the fuck up. He hopes that the promise of a comic will keep her quiet on the bus while he works out the various drops. It's a long bus ride into central London.

'Billy, can we go upstairs and sit right at the front? Can we?'

Poor kid's so excited. Anyone would think she's never been on a fuckin' bus before. Billy is left with no choice but to sound like a caring, fatherly person.

'Course we can, darling,' he says, with as much fake enthusiasm as he can muster.

He remembers to look up every now and then when she points out every damn thing she can see from the front of the bus. 'Yeah, amazing, clever girl,' but soon tires of the role. It seems as if she wants to identify every church, tree and shop on the route and Billy really doesn't have the bandwidth for it. 'Why don't you read your comic I got you?'

Candace does as she's told, which gives him a few minutes to scroll his phone, checking that operations are running smoothly, and think about the day. The kitchen is on track and manufacturing crack at a good pace. Lorna is off her head – out the way. Billy promises himself a shag later when the kitchen crew have gone. The peace doesn't last long, though. After looking at a couple of pages, she puts the comic down on her lap.

'I feel sick.'

He turns away and rolls his eyes, but manages to control his mouth from saying what he's thinking. Instead he says, 'Ah, do ya, darlin'? That's a shame. Well, take deep breaths. It's not long now.'

Billy doesn't take any chances. He is too senior in the chain to make a rookie error and make themselves really conspicuous, so they get off early in Clapham and change buses to get more central. It's just a short ride then on the underground to the West End. First stop is Oxford Street, to the toy section of a department store where he's making a delivery of cocaine and ketamine. What's more natural than taking a five-year-old in there? Candace is the perfect cover. He doesn't ask questions. He's not interested in who people are or what they do. It's all very quick. He meets the men in hoodies near some stairs, opening Candace's rucksack and rummaging around for what he needs while it's still strapped to her back.

Job done.

Except he hasn't stopped to think about the impact of taking a deprived kid inside a toy store.

Billy holds her hand and pulls her towards the door, but Candace isn't ready to leave. The shop is busy with people buying toys for children. He tugs her hand as she tries to stop when they walk by the circular shelves, piled high with soft toys. She sees something, a teddy of some sort and calls out, 'Stiiiitch!'

She's so loud that people nearby notice her and smile. An American tourist says, 'Lucky girl. Is Daddy going to get Stitch for you?'

Billy grimaces, quickly turning his expression into a

smile when he realises that he has to keep the attention away from them.

Stupid kid has the memory of Billy buying her a milkshake, no doubt. 'You want a teddy, Candy?'

Candace looks as if all her Christmases have come at once as she takes the small teddy and they walk over to the checkout. She holds the stupid thing tight to her chest. Billy is pissed off. It isn't the money; money's no problem. He just doesn't want any distinguishing features in case anything goes wrong and the police ask for witnesses. He does a quick calculation.

Small girl, pink rucksack, cream baseball cap carrying a blue Stitch teddy bear. There's a lot of detail there. Too much. He'll try to ditch the teddy as soon as he can.

Next stop is Mayfair. The galleries are usually full of former public school kids, or their international equivalents, networking, socialising and meeting for business. These people love a bit of coke. They walk up to the front door of one, where a very handsome, tanned and quintessentially Englishman in a dark blue suit with a crisp, white shirt but no tie, comes over to them. Billy carefully looks left and right to make sure no one's looking. He has already stashed the drugs for this drop in the zipper pocket at the front of Candace's bag. He hands over the cocaine wraps to the man, whose accent is a million miles away from Billy's and puts the thick wedge of cash in used twenties and fifties into his own bag, strapped across his body.

'Come on now, kid.' He tugs Candace's rucksack straps

to leave, she drops her head down and hugs her teddy even more tightly into her chest, dragging her feet.

As they cross the smart Mayfair street he feels as if he's pulling her along. This won't do. The fuckin' kid needs to sort it out. He's not putting up with this bollocks. A couple are walking the other way, which prompts a return to his happy, jolly caring voice when he clocks them.

'Are you hungry?'

Candace lifts her head and smiles and nods. 'Yessss!'

Billy looks around for the nearest solution. He can only see posh sandwich shops selling expensive pastrami and other crap.

'Do you fancy McDonald's?'

Candace nods enthusiastically.

Billy checks his phone, there isn't one nearby. He locates a Shake Shack, drops a pin and begins to walk in the direction of the place. He glances back to the gallery, just to check.

Something's up. He can feel it.

Billy is very good at keeping his wits about him. He looks in the shop windows as they walk, to see if anyone is following. He can't really tell. He just feels slightly edgy. He keeps hold of Candace's hand the whole time. He doesn't care about her, but he cares very much about the contents of her backpack.

They get some food, Candace at first complaining that it isn't actually McDonald's, but appeased when she sees the burgers and fries. Now she wants to go to the toilet.

He hasn't factored any of this shit in. He's never spent this much time alone with a kid. He tells her to wait. Then, after the food, he walks her to the toilet and waits outside with the backpack while she does what she needs to do. He realises with a start that he must have left the meal deal paperwork on the stairs in the toy department as he was going through her bag. That was careless.

He needs to find something else to lay on top, like a coat, or jumper, or something else soft. On the way back to the tube he spots an H&M store and heads in to find something to put in the rucksack. He still has a tight grip of her hand as they walk through the children's section. She runs up to a sparkling pink and lilac party dress.

'Like on Strictly!' she squeals. She picks it off the rail. 'Can I have this? Can I?'

It wasn't exactly what Billy had in mind, but now Candace is pleading loudly with him. And a shop assistant is nearby.

'Wow, you'd look like a princess in that,' she says, rather unhelpfully, in Billy's opinion. Why do people feel like they have a fuckin' invitation to join the conversation.

On the other hand, it's only £30 and it can sit on top of the drugs, easy to lift out. And the kid wants the bloody thing.

'Yeah, okay, Candy. But no more asking for anything else today, okay? 'Cos I'm telling you, you ain't gonna get it.'

Candace nods compliantly and skips with Billy to the

checkout. He has the dress laid out across his arm. He pays for it and is about to put it in her rucksack when he hears a man's voice behind him.

'Playing Daddy, are we?'

It's Ricky. Another ex-con from a different gang who he'd known – and despised – in prison. Just the sort of person he doesn't want to bump into.

Ricky leans in and whispers in Billy's ear. 'Fuck off back to your shithole and stay away from town, yeah?'

Billy looks at him and decides against his first choice of response. 'Yeah, sure. That's great, good to see you, Ricky. You take care,' and directs Candace out of the shop ahead of him. They're heading back in the direction of Oxford Circus, but Billy knows now that he's being followed. Instead of going in the direction he actually *needs* to, he walks into the tube and they jump on a Victoria Line train to King's Cross, then he walks out of the front of the station and catches a taxi back to the West End. A pain in the arse, but it's got to be done. You can't be too careful.

He finishes the other five drop-offs scheduled for the day, at various businesses and a big hotel. He has 15k stashed in his bag now and he needs to get back home. Even though he's given the kid everything she bloody wants, Candace is grumpy, she's tired. Billy is pissed off. Being with her all day has been hard work. She's a whingeing, whining bag of nuisance and, from tomorrow onwards, Joey can do the fuckin' run. Especially as he's been clocked now.

After the final drop, they get on the bus towards the flats.

It's dark by the time they get off. No messages from Lorna. Billy thinks again how easy it is to take over a smackhead's kid. By now he no longer feels the need to hold onto Candace's grubby little hand. Instead he walks on at his usual pace and tells her to keep up.

'We haven't got all day.'

'It's night time,' she says, her voice petulant.

They walk past the Co-op, Billy muttering to himself. He'd thought it would be easy to use Candace as the perfect cover, but it's a nightmare dealing with a kid all day. They're so fuckin' demanding. Part of him doesn't know how he's managed to get through it, but he did his business and that's chill, that's all that matters. Joey can do it from now on.

As they pass the bookies, there's a sound behind him. He turns and just sees the glint of a knife in the moonlight.

VIII

Billy

He feels the pain in his side a second or two after the blade strikes home. The two men who jumped him are black shadows, already disappearing back into the darkness as he collapses onto the pavement. Fuckers! His guard was down. He should have been more careful. Breathing heavily, he manages to drag himself up onto his feet and limp to a bench outside the library. The kid won't have had a clue what's just happened. They were too quick.

'Sit down here,' he tells Candace, indicating the space next to him on the bench. 'Get my phone out of my pocket and pass it to me.'

'What did those men want?' Candace asks, worriedly looking back at the direction they ran off in.

'Nothing. Nothing. Forget it. I think they just ran into me. It was an accident.'

Billy is a master at keeping his head down and keeping a low profile. Even with a stab wound that really needs medical intervention, he knows that if he sits on this bench with Candace and manages to stay upright, he will not cause any unwanted attention. They'll get away with it. Because what other choice does he have? With this much money, a small kid and residual drugs in her backpack, there's only one way it would go if the authorities were to get involved. He applies pressure to the wound, trying to stop the blood flow.

Thank fuck for Joey. The man has his uses. It takes only a few minutes for Joey to appear. They communicate with nods as Joey quickly and discreetly checks Billy over and discovers the stab wound.

'You okay?' Joey asks Candace.

'What are you asking her for?' Billy hisses. The pain is excruciating, as Joey hoists him up into a standing position.

Candace shakes her head.

'Let me carry your rucksack.'

Joey puts the rucksack across his shoulder while balancing Billy's weight. They walk along with Joey holding Billy up and holding Candace's hand on the other side. To passers-by, it probably looks like Billy has had too much to drink, holding his side because he feels nauseous. And little kids out late at night is not a rare sight in this neck of the woods. They reach the flats. Joey presses the lift button.

Even Candace is surprised when it shudders into life. 'The lift is working!'

They get up to Billy's floor and, with Joey's help, he makes it to the front door.

'Is Billy alright?' Candace asks.

'Just tired, darling,' Billy manages, with a groan.

Joey helps Billy to settle himself on the sofa and switches on the TV for Candace, pulling the armchair forward so that she is closer to the telly and not looking behind.

Billy needs Joey to take a good look at the cut. He thinks he's escaped the worst, but it's hard to tell. He's been stabbed before and survived. In prison they learn the best places to stab someone to achieve what needs to be done, whether that's as a warning or to be fatal. Billy knows where the vital organs are and which blood arteries do what. So does Joey. They're good at medical stuff, because they need to be.

This wound is a warning.

'Kit's in the bathroom,' Billy grunts.

Joey returns quickly with towels and the medical box. Billy's not daft. The box is loaded with sterilisers, plasters, skin wound strips and bandages.

Joey puts Billy back together while Candace watches TV.

'You'll live,' he says.

Billy nods and grimaces.

'Something to eat?'

Billy asks for a ham and mustard sandwich and a mug of tea. 'And a truckload of painkillers.'

'Do you wanna sandwich, Candace?' Joey asks. 'Ham sandwich?'

She nods to that.

'With mustard?'

'What's that?'

Candace: The Gallery Girl

Joey explains that it's yellow and spicy tasting. He's got some patience, that's for sure. While Billy's just about done with the kid.

Candace makes a face and shakes her head. 'No mutard.' The backpack is on the floor. Candace reaches for it and pulls out the H&M bag from the top. She lifts out her dress and holds it up.

'Look what Billy bought me.'

'That's generous of him.'

She also holds up the Stitch toy.

Joey raises an eyebrow and Billy shrugs.

Patched up, Billy needs help getting to his room and into bed. Joey offers his shoulder once more. 'You gonna be alright?'

'Nothing that a bit of paracetamol and some spliff won't sort, I reckon.'

'I'm impressed with that dress, mate. Tell you what, you've made a little girl very happy. Thought you were a hard-nosed bastard. Didn't know you had a soft streak.'

'Fuck that,' Billy says. 'You can work with her from now on, and I tell you now, she needs to understand that she can't have stuff all the time. She made my life fuckin' hell.'

'I think someone else was trying to make it worse. Who d'you reckon cut ya then?'

Billy sighs. He's pretty sure he knows. Ricky is his nearest rival. Billy has a wider and financially more lucrative operation than Ricky and he knows how much Ricky hates that. 'Ricky! He was following me from Mayfair, I reckon. I felt that something weren't right. You know, you get that sixth sense sometimes. Then when we were in the shop, buying the little princess her dress, he was standing next to me at the till. Arsehole.'

'Ricky?' Joey also knows Ricky from prison. He whistles. 'So he's out, is he?'

'Yeah, but we're not gonna worry about that. Ricky doesn't worry me. What's more important is that the kid is useful. It's brilliant. You can move around freely. No one as much as looks twice in your direction. They can't see what's right under their fuckin' noses. No one says anything. Other than when she wants something, that is, and then they join in and don't seem to be able to keep their fuckin' mouths shut. It's fuckin' weird and annoying. People can't keep their beaks out, can they?'

'Well, she's a working kid now. It would be nice to give her a bit of reward. Nothing much. A bit of pocket money?'

Billy laughs. 'Nah, no need. You said it exactly. She's a working kid. Not to be confused with a normal kid. No more treats. She needs to be trained up good and proper from now on. She's got to learn to be obedient. She needs a firm hand.'

'Yeah, but she's put in a shift, today,' Joey insists. 'If she's working all the time, she'll need some payment. That's fairs?'

'Fuck that. Kids don't get paid. D'you hear me?' He pauses. 'And don't fuckin' talk to me about what's fair!'

IX

Joey

Joey lifts a sleeping Candace, still clutching her sparkly dress, from her upright position in the chair and lays her down gently on the sofa. He pries her dress from her hands and spreads it across the back of the sofa so it doesn't get crumpled. He fetches a blanket from the airing cupboard and puts it over her. He checks on Billy again, then heads out of the flat and downstairs to Lorna's to see what's going on there.

There's no need to use his key. He walks straight in because no one has locked the door. Lorna is in her kitchen, dressed in a grubby, off-white T-shirt and shorts, pouring a Red Bull into a plastic cup. The giant red cherry on the front of her shirt looks ridiculous.

There is no sign of the cooks, they've already packed up and gone home for the day.

'You seen Candy? She went to school today. She's a proper big girl now.' Lorna says, proudly.

Does she really believe that? Joey feels some pity for Lorna. It's cruel, how easy it's been for Billy to exploit her. On the other hand, she's a shit mother. A drug addict whose entire relationship with her daughter is transactional. He's already seen how she uses Candace because she can't manage without her. Lorna even used Candace to lure Billy in, though she didn't exactly have to try, he'd already set his sights on her and her daughter. But what kind of mother does that?

He finds himself comparing his own situation again. He was raised by a good woman, a caring woman, who just couldn't deal with County Lines and Joey's spiralling, out-of-control behaviour and attitude. Deep down, Joey loves his mum. He misses her. But it wouldn't be fair to see her again until he's out of the crime world. And that's unlikely. It's hard to leave. There are no easy ways out.

When they're young they're told: *to leave, you have to die or leave the country.* It's not much of a choice. Given the debt bondage, who can get the kind of money together that it would take to go abroad? Permanently. Anyway, he knew what he was getting into.

Or did he?

The question is, does he really want to be part of inflicting that same sentence on another innocent kid? Candace is way younger than he was. He's more than aware that he and Billy, and this whole world they've dragged her into, will turn Candace into a criminal. There's no escape. She's so young. By the time she's a young woman, she'll only ever have known crime. She will be very good at it by then, he has no doubt. And that means being devoid of empathy or a conscience.

'Candace is asleep upstairs. She's had a busy day.'

'She alright, though?'

Joey looks away. 'Yeah, it all went well. She's good, fast asleep. Billy's laid up today and tomorrow, so I'll keep an eye on her tomorrow.'

Lorna nods, vacantly and takes a sip from her cup, hands shaking. She's so thin and pale he can almost see through her. She looks as if she's been cut out from a sheet of baking paper.

'Lorna, when did you last eat?'

She makes a sour face. 'Dunno.'

'You should try and eat something.' Joey looks around the kitchen. The cooks have put everything away and the place is spotless. They're very good at what they do and keep a tidy kitchen, there's no doubt about that. Which is kind of funny, considering what it is they do. Beyond the kitchen, he can see that the side light is on in the lounge. In this light, and from an angle that obscures the chaos, the flat doesn't look too depressing. It could be nice, with a bit of effort.

Except that there's a lot of mess in the lounge. It's a shithole in there. Piles of Domino's boxes, the remnants of multiple take-aways and half-drunk bottles of Pepsi Max. There are overflowing ashtrays on every surface. Discarded clothes nestle with empty crisp packets. A dead plant in one corner. It looks like what it is: the home of a junkie. It smells so bad. But it wouldn't take an awful lot to sort out. Joey goes to fetch a bin bag from under the sink, but there isn't any. He tries a couple of drawers, but there really isn't anything other than a really old roll of clingfilm. He checks in the fridge. There's a carton of milk on a shelf inside, but when he takes the lid off, the smell is rancid. He throws it away. There isn't any bread left.

'I'll go to the shop and get some food.'

He wonders how Candace manages to eat, how meals can be made from nothing. A growing kid needs the right foods. None of this is right. He reminds himself that Candace is not his kid. He's not responsible for her. Under Billy's definition, she's not even a kid. She's a worker, a mule. But it's hard to have the image of that little sleeping girl and her sparkly dress in his head and think of her as a mule. Everything is so fucked up.

Lorna pads back to the sitting room and settles herself back on the sofa. She pulls at her hair around her face. Joey turns to leave. He hates this place and everything it represents. He closes the door behind him, making sure that the latch is down and nobody else can just walk in, like he did. It doesn't guarantee safety though. He has a key, the cooks have keys, and God knows who else now has keys to this flat.

In the morning, Joey's up early and when he walks into the sitting room, Candace bounces off the sofa over to him. She's wearing her new dress and spins around smiling.

'I'm a princess!'

Billy walks in from his bedroom. He's wincing with every step. The pain relief of two paracetamol every four hours, plus spliff to take the edge off, evidently isn't quite enough. Clearly he's forgotten about Candace, though, because he looks at her crossly.

'What's she doing here? She lives downstairs.'

Joey smiles at Candace. 'She was fast asleep so I left her. She's good. She's fine. She's not doing any harm. She's just a kid.'

Billy walks toward the kitchen and Joey follows, closing the door behind him. Billy goes to the fridge and pulls out a carton of orange juice. Joey watches as Billy drinks straight from the carton.

'She's not a kid, Joey. She's a working mule. How many times do I have to tell you? Don't get these things confused or you'll end up being cut or killed.' He stares at Joey, narrowing his eyes. 'Do not get soft on me, Joe. You'll die out there if you're soft. Look what happened to me yesterday.'

Joey listens. 'Yeah, mate. I know.'

An hour later, Joey arrives at Lorna's flat with Candace and a couple of bags of shopping. He loads up the fridge and puts the cereal packets on the side near the toaster.

'Mummy, Mummy, look. We have food!'

The kid is beside herself with excitement, dressed in her sparkly dress and clutching her toy Stitch.

There's no response from her mum, though. All they can hear is Lorna retching from the bathroom.

Candace tries again. 'Mummy, look what Billy bought me.'

Lorna suddenly appears from the bathroom. 'Oh yeah, let's see.'

Candace pushes Stitch in front of Lorna's face. She pulls out the skirt of her dress and does a twirl.

'Candy-girl, you look beautiful. Aww, look at my baby. You look so good!'

Candace is full of tales of her adventures. She tells about how they went to a restaurant and had chicken and chips and ice cream.

'Billy's spoiling you,' Lorna says, but she seems pleased. 'Where is he?'

'He's laid up. I told you last night—' Joey breaks off, realising that she doesn't remember. She would have been high, too far gone to take in any information.

'Who are they?' Candace asks with a frown, as the cooks arrive and put music on as they set up.

'The cooks,' Joey answers, momentarily caught off-guard. He realises his mistake when Candace starts asking more questions. She's curious, wants to know what they're cooking and whether she can have some. It starts to strike Joey just what a highly dangerous setting this kid is in. She's too inquisitive. He doesn't want to leave her here. The cooks are indifferent. They don't give a fuck if she lives or dies. This is pure business, there are no emotions involved. He thinks about how he can pitch it to Billy. Their asset, their little slave girl, Candy, might become ill or die – which would not be good for business. It wouldn't be good for anyone.

Joey leaves Candace on the sofa, tells her that the kitchen is out of bounds, and heads back up to the flat above.

'What's happening?'

Billy is back in bed and keen to know that the day's work is underway. 'Cooks there?'

Joey reassures him that all is well. He doesn't know how to raise his concerns about Candace with Billy. He can't come out with it directly. Billy will just accuse him of going soft again. Billy will only ever have his eye on the prize. Everything and everyone else are a means to an end.

'Candace will be alright, I reckon, if she stays away from the kitchen and the door,' he says. He emphasises the latter, but doesn't say anymore. He's just sowing a seed for now.

To his surprise, Billy takes the bait. After spending a day with Candace, maybe he understands a bit more that kids don't always do as they are told.

'She's the kid of a junkie, she's probably fucked like her mum,' Billy says.

Joey agrees with him, knowing that's the best thing to do. Billy looks thoughtful. Joey knows he needs to pick his moments and let Billy think that keeping Candace safer is his idea. The conversation moves on. The focus is on Candace's ability to move the drugs across town without raising suspicion.

'She needs some more clothes and a baseball cap in a

different colour. Also a new backpack, nothing that sticks out from the crowd. She's got to blend in. You up for a trip to the shops?'

Joey nods. He heads straight off and finds a new backpack in Lidl. This one is lilac with an iridescent unicorn in the middle. He sees a lilac baseball cap, also with a unicorn printed centre-front, above the peak of the cap, as if Candace will be starting a new career at Unicorns PLC, he thinks to himself.

Joey goes straight to Lorna's flat to show Candace her new gear. Billy must be hurting less than he was first thing this morning, because he comes out of Lorna's bedroom with a smirk on his face, grabbing his penis through his jeans.

'That's better. I needed that,' he says to Joey with a wink.

Joey wishes that he wouldn't talk like that when the kid can hear. She isn't safe here, even from Billy, he suspects. Joey can't stand the sight of Lorna, either. He finds her repulsive, mainly for not protecting and looking after her daughter, but also for giving in to Billy so easily.

They walk through to the lounge, where Candace is sitting. Billy can see for himself what a mess the place is in — apart from the requisitioned kitchen.

'Aright, Candy-girl?' Billy says.

Candace nods and carries on twiddling Stitch's nose around. In spite of the nod, she seems unhappy. Perhaps she knows, intuitively, that it's not safe anymore. Perhaps it no longer feels like her home.

'More adventures for you, today, yeah? But this time you're gonna go out with Joey. Look, he's bought you new stuff.'

Candace turns and looks up at Joey, eyes bright again. She reaches for Joey's hand.

Billy frowns and quietly reminds Joey that she's a mule and that he does the jobs and then comes back. 'No messing around, right?'

In some ways, it's all to the good. Ricky's gang don't know Joey and they wouldn't have taken much notice of Candace on that last outing. With new clothes, backpack and cap to disguise her in, they won't make any connection. And Joey and Candace look similar enough. It's a better fit than walking around with Billy. More natural.

Joey has a different delivery run to do. Yesterday it was the business in the West End, today it's private houses in the north of London – around Camden, Highgate and Hampstead. Lots of celebrities live there, musos, media types and TV personalities. They like their coke, Joey knows. Joey layers up Candace's new rucksack using paper dividers for each postcode. At the bottom is the crack and some fentanyl, a potent, synthetic opioid, way more powerful than morphine: one of the regulars likes to risk death in the pursuit of creative ideas – and it's a tasty little pop at £50 per pill.

The propaganda is that it's a drug that hasn't left America yet, that it's not in the UK. But it's been cooking and available in the UK for several years. There's not enough being said in the mainstream media and it seems the government and the police aren't doing enough to tell people what's really going on. Most of the population would freak out if they knew.

Candace is ready, playing her part perfectly as a regular little girl dressed for a day out. On Billy's advice, Joey packs a hoodie at the top of the rucksack, hiding all the gear, just in case the pack is opened in front of people who might raise the alarm. Keep it all looking as normal as possible, that's the motto.

'All set?' Joey asks. Candace nods and calls out to her mum, 'Bye!'

Lorna is oblivious. She's out of it, lying on her bed with her knickers by her feet, probably totally unaware that she has even had sex.

Billy sits in the chair on his phone but breaks off to say, 'You two have a good day now.'

'We will. Bye Billy!' Candace says, and skips off holding Joey's hand.

Joey

By lunchtime, they've done all the big houses on the list. They're ahead of schedule and have time to walk through the cemetery and sit down to eat their meal deals. Candace sits on the bench and swings her legs as she chews on her sandwich. She asks loads of questions about where they are.

'What's a cemetery?'

When Joey explains, it transpires that she didn't know that people came to places like this when they died.

'I thought they went to heaven.'

'Well, yeah, some do, I guess,' Joe is wrongfooted.

'So what happens when you die?'

Joey can't answer that one. Talking to a kid is complicated.

After they've eaten, Joey puts the rubbish in a bin and they take a little walk around looking at some of the gravestones. Joey explains that it's been used in some films and finds himself promising to watch the *Fantastic Beasts* movies with her. Billy's right. He is soft. He tells Candace that some famous people are buried here.

'Lots of artists and writers.'

'What's a writer?'

Jesus, she asks a lot of questions.

'Well, you know when you read books—'

Candace shakes her head. 'I don't know how to do that. Mummy said she'd show me, but she hasn't.'

Fuck sake. And of course, Candace hasn't ever been to school to be able to learn. Joey finds himself showing her letters of the alphabet on some of the gravestones and monuments. She's a fast learner. They get through ABCD and E. She also likes some of the sculptures on the monuments. And likes spotting the word 'DEAD' carved into one artist's grave.

'Now you only need two more letters to be able to write your name. But that's enough for today. We've got some more visits to do.'

They walk out of Highgate cemetery and towards a council estate. This is the bit Joey is less keen to go near with the kid in tow. But he knows that the surroundings will feel more familiar to Candace. It's not too dissimilar to where they live. They sit down together on another bench in a side-street near the flats. It's a safe bench, not in sight of the CCTV. All this stuff is worked out in advance by the gang, who have insiders in the police who advise which areas are without cameras. Sometimes they even have people inside the town councils who own the cameras. It only takes one person to turn a camera off and no one really knows. When the cameras are off there's no evidence. Billy laughs at how easy all this is. Easy for him, perhaps, at his level in the organisation, but not so much for the kids who end up messed up or dead. That word 'DEAD' seems to be following Joey around today.

He shivers, though it's nice and warm.

His mum used to say that feeling was 'someone walking over your grave'.

He leaves Candace on the bench, while he walks a few yards with her backpack. They're at the bottom layer now, crack to the nitties, the addicts who crawl in like two-legged spiders and scuttle away with their wrap, back into their hellish lives. They're always the same sad faces. Often a mum, a young mum, pregnant or with a buggy. He's reminded of Lorna. The children of crackheads always look flat-faced and often their hands stim; the jerky, repetitive movements are a dead giveaway. They are usually malnourished and tired looking. It's hardly surprising when they must be living a life of neglect due to their parent's addiction. It's amazing that Candace has stayed as healthy looking as she has. She's clearly a survivor.

As he doles out the goods, Joey always asks himself why these kids are still with their mothers. Why someone hasn't intervened to help them. But he and Billy have discussed it before. You have a lot of time to talk in prison. They know that there are hardly any foster carers left these days to look after them. There's hardly any money in welfare, so the babies hang on in there. Somehow. He wonders how many die. Joey has one eye on Candace, making sure she's okay over there on the bench, hasn't wandered off. She's fine, she's found a cat to talk to. He finishes up and pulls the zip on her backpack closed after he folds her hoodie and puts it back in. Now it really is just a little girl's rucksack again. There are no drugs left. He messages Billy. *Mission complete, coming back to base camp.*

At Billy's suggestion, Joey makes up a bed for Candy in their flat.

Both men agree that she needs to be fit for work, though Joey knows they're coming at that decision for very different reasons. She needs to be 'seen' to be happy and loved – otherwise questions could be asked. The last thing they need is social services poking their beaks in.

'I'll make a little area for her in the sitting room, behind a bookshelf, so she has her own space.'

The men never party or have people back to their flat, so it won't impact what passes for a social life. Lorna's flat is now for business, and Lorna is for Billy to shag. As far as Billy is concerned, it's easier to do that if the kid's up here.

In the morning, Candace bounces into the kitchen. She jumps up onto the sink drainer to look out of the window and sees Joey doing exercises on the balcony. She jumps back down and opens the door.

'Morning, Joey. Am I seeing Mummy today?'

'Yeah, sure, if you want?'

Candace shakes her head. Interesting. She doesn't want to see her mum. Perhaps it's not so surprising under the circumstances. Poor kid.

'Are we going out?' she asks.

'Yes, we are, but breakfast first.'

Joey realises that he's left most of the food he bought for Lorna and Candace back in their flat.

'Frosties or Shreddies?' he asks.

Candace calls out, 'Frosties, please.'

He runs down to Lorna's place to get them. Candace will need some energy. Today the drop offs are in Brighton. While Candace is eating, Joey books a taxi to the train station. All expenses paid today. Brighton is good business. There are other gangs there, of course, but the clients know Billy and have been using his services for a while. He has a reputation for reasonable prices and good shit.

It's mostly cocaine in Brighton, but some of his clients in the LGBTQI+ community enjoy chem sex and like mephedrone, GHB, GBL and alkyl nitrites, or poppers. G can make them feel euphoric. Combine that with a loss of inhibitions, increased confidence, and a higher sex drive, and you have a winner. It's always been a steady business in this part of the world.

More recently, the clients seem to have acquired a taste for ketamine. Billy's good at bowing to what the market wants. Joey knows that today's day out will see a return of approximately 8k. Billy likes to keep these clients happy, because when it comes to festivals, celebrations and parties, that figure can easily double.

Joey and Candace do some more letters on the train,

to pass the time. Candace is delighted with being able to write her own name.

She's also excited to be by the seaside. The drop-offs are all in a walkable area. Some are workers in the shops, pubs and restaurants. It doesn't take too long. They sit outside a café in the sunshine and have a late lunch. Toasted sandwiches today, and Candace has a chocolate milkshake which she drinks through two long straws.

'Joey?' she says, between slurps of the thick shake.

'Hmmm?'

'I'm very happy.'

'That's good.' He loves hearing that. And she does seem happy, Joey thinks. After their lunch they head off to the Sealife Centre. She deserves a treat after all the walking about she's done today.

Candace has never seen anything like it before. It's worth the entrance price just to see her delight as they play with fish in the tanks near the entrance. They have some rock pools where you can interact with some of the starfish and crabs. Then they walk around the rest of the place, looking at the multitude of sea creatures in their tanks: little sharks, a playful octopus and a graceful sea turtle. Her joy is infectious and Joey feels warm inside as he watches it. He can't imagine that Lorna, given the state of her, has ever taken Candace to somewhere like this. More interested in scoring her next hit than in spending time with her kid. On the way out they head towards the gift shop where Candace chooses a little whale.

'I'm gonna call him JoJo,' she says. 'Like you.'

It's ridiculous, but Joey's strangely pleased by it. There's still time in the day and heat in the sun when they come back outside, so they head to the beach. They take their shoes and socks off and have a paddle. Then they head over to the pier for some more fun. Candace's eyes go wide at the different rides and slot machines.

They sit on the beach with a bag of chips, fighting off the seagulls who want to join them for dinner. Candace finds this hysterical, and nicknames the boldest one 'Mr Bananas'. Joey laughs, she must have heard someone talking about Billy…

As the sun begins to set, Candace leans into Joey, they sit staring out to sea for a while, saying nothing. Candace is utterly worn out. She yawns and closes her eyes. Joey calls an Uber and they head toward the station for their train. Candace sleeps against Joey all the way. He puts his arm around her to keep her safe. He likes the fact that they look like father and daughter. He stares at her innocent features as they soften in sleep and feels a pang of fear. It's ridiculous to think he can keep her safe.

In the morning, the rows begin. Joey defends himself.

'You bought her a toy, too. You bought her the Stitch thing.'

'Because I *had* to. We were in a fuckin' toy store. And she didn't name it after me. Not like Mr Fuckin' Sealife Centre over here.'

Candace is watching TV. Billy has followed Joey into the

kitchen so that they can carry on arguing about how much Joey has been spoiling Candace.

'You need to back off from the kid. She's a mule, a business proposition. Nothing more. She's totally disposable just like her twat of a mother.'

The words are already sounding tired. Billy's like a broken record. But he won't shut up. Joey remains quiet. Billy is becoming very happy with the set-up. It's already profitable. They'll be able to keep clearing over 100k a week with the various routes and little operations he's got set up across the area. Candace is his golden egg and he doesn't want anything to interfere with that.

Billy gets right up close to his face, so close that Joey can smell the fags and last night's burger. 'Mate, she's a fuckin' slave, a worker. Never forget that. If you get too involved, you'll fuck up everything.'

Joey pushes him away.

'Yeah, mate. I get ya. I hear ya, it's okay. I'm just keeping her in good nick so she works well. Don't worry, I'm not the daddy type.'

Billy pats him on the shoulder. 'Good,' he nods approvingly. 'That's more like it. She's just for business. When we're done here, in six months or so, we'll leave her and Lorna to get back to their fucked up lives. Just keep it chill till then, yeah?'

Joey tells himself that Billy is right. He does need to take a step back. He doesn't want to get emotionally involved with Candace. Besides, Billy is not someone you

Candace: The Gallery Girl

piss off. He hasn't earned that nickname, 'Bananas', for nothing. Joey has no intention of stepping out of line. He needs to be on the right side of Billy or his life won't be worth living. Or he'll wind up dead. Drowned in a river. That's what happens if you cross the boss. Joey knows it. Everyone knows it. Except Ricky. Billy's rival is the only psycho stupid enough to tug Billy's chain. They hate each other and watch each other's every move the whole time, ready to pounce at the first sign of weakness.

'Well, to help keep things as they should be, I'm switching things up a bit.' Billy lets Joey know that, from now on, Ank will be working with Candace. Joey remembers meeting Ank, short for 'Anchor' a while back, but doesn't know the guy well. He's young, only 19 years old and, like everyone else, has been glued into County Lines since he was a little kid. Probably not as young as Candace though. Joey is going to pair up with Carlos, also just out of prison for a different part of the operation.

Joey knows Billy has him sussed and he's been outflanked as far as Candace is concerned.

'Is Ank a nonce?' he asks, before he can help himself.

'I dunno, mate. He has a little sister. No idea if he fucks her or not.'

Joey tells himself to let go of Candace. She is not his responsibility. She's nothing to do with him. It's not his job to keep her safe.

There's more. 'Candy needs to be with her mum back in

the flat, in case neighbours get suspicious. Move her stuff down, now!'

This bit is hard for Joey, but he keeps telling himself that Candace is nothing to do with him, that he's too soft, she is just business.

Deep down, though, he knows that's not true.

XI

Joey

It doesn't work out with Ank. Joey is called by Billy to do some more work with Candy; she's refusing to go out with her new 'handler'.

'She trusts you, so I want you to reassure Candy that Ank is *your friend*. Go out with her, all together, to the park or something and let her see you *like* Ank, yeah?'

It doesn't escape Joey's notice that this feels a bit like what social workers do when they want people to adopt a child. So Joey turns this back onto Billy for a laugh. 'Do you want me to write up a fucking care plan with all her favourite food, drinks and TV programmes?'

'Nah,' Billy says. 'Fuck off. Just get that kid to like Ank. We need her out working. Carlos will have to do today's deliveries while you play the starring role in Three Men and a fuckin' Baby!'

'Yeah, but that ain't three, Billy. There's two of us. You sure your maths is okay?'

Billy laughs at that. 'Fuck off.'

Joey feels relieved that things are back on a better footing with Billy. He'd had a mild panic that Billy was onto him and that was going to make his life very difficult. But that moment seems to have passed. Anyway, a few days away and he's stopped thinking about Candace so much. He'll just do his bit to help Ank take over.

Joey goes down to the flat. In his mind, it's become flat 2. He's stopped calling it Lorna's flat, because she's no longer in charge. It's busy with tall men in hoodies, measuring out and loading up bags. Billy is with Ank. Ank is pleased to see Joey. They give each other a pound hug – a handshake with a one-armed hug, followed by a friendly pat on the back.

'Bro.'

'Enough with the love-in,' Billy says. 'Princess Candy is in her room.'

Joey and Ank head to her door. Joey knocks first and when they go in, Candace is sitting on her bed.

'JoJo!' Her face lights up into a big smile.

Joey blushes and hopes Billy didn't hear that.

'Hey, Candy, I want you to meet my very good friend, Ank, here. Do you want to come out today and go to the park with us, get an ice cream?'

Candace is already sliding off the bed. 'Yes, please. Can we go now?'

She pushes through the two men. Joey laughs and looks at Ank. 'I think that means the lady is ready to go.'

Joey takes the opportunity to check on Lorna. He walks past her room and opens the door, just a crack. He sees

Lorna sleeping on her side, her long T-shirt pulled up, her shorts next to her feet. He knows that Lorna is being used by Billy, and probably others in this flat. It makes him feel ashamed to be male. But he's also frustrated with her for not seeing this situation coming.

Billy catches him at the door and raises an eyebrow. 'You wanna ride, Joey?'

Joey pulls the door shut and smiles. 'Nah, mate. I'm good.' He makes his way along the hall. 'Okay, Candy, Anchor, let's go to the park.'

The heads of the other gang members in the kitchen and lounge turn.

'Why does this trap house sound more like a fuckin' kindergarten?' one snorts.

'Bye, everyone,' Candace waves.

Perhaps against their better judgement a couple of them find themselves waving back and saying 'Byeee.'

As they close the door behind them, Joey hears Billy tell them to, 'Shut the fuck up, you cunts, and get back to work!'

Candy holds Joey's hand as they walk.

Ank looks at this. 'Should I hold her hand like that when we're out? Is that allowed?'

'If she wants to. It's better that you do, it looks more natural. Like you're her dad.'

Ank looks confused. 'I fink I'm a bit young, man, to be her dad.'

Joey shrugs. 'Not round here.'

'Tell me again why Billy is working little kids?'

'It's the best cover. They're easy. No one suspects a little kid to be carrying drugs. You can go anywhere. If you can get the kids to look natural, then no one suspects. We just glide through town unnoticed.' Joey gives the explanation, but he's beginning to wonder himself if it's so much of a good idea. It feels so wrong.

'Yeah, cool, I get it. So all I need to do is be like a nice uncle.'

'Something like that.' Joey tries to ignore the little stab of jealousy he feels.

They walk through the park gate and straightaway Candy sees the ice cream van. She jumps up and down on the spot.

'Ice cream! Can I have an ice cream, JoJo?'

'Sure, Candy, what flavour d'ya want?'

In her haste to reach the van, she slips and falls over. There are immediate tears.

Ank says, 'Candy, get up, there ain't nuffin' wrong, girl.'

Joey reaches down and helps her stand up, brushing the dirt from her knees. Candace reaches out for Joey to hug. He kneels down and she leans into him. Her crazy, corkscrew hair tickles his face as he hugs her. 'There, you go. You're all good.'

He lifts her up and carries her to the ice cream van. 'You can have whatever you want.' He turns her around so she can see the ice cream pictures. The tears have subsided, but she shows no sign of wanting to get down.

'Which one you tryin' to point at? The Mr Whippy?' Ank asks. He sounds frustrated.

She nods.

Joey carefully puts her down on the ground. 'With a flake?'

She nods again.

'And sauce?'

Another nod. 'Chocolate,' she whispers.

Joey laughs and repeats the order back through the serving hatch. 'Mr Whippy, two flakes and chocolate sauce, please.'

Candace smiles.

'Ank, you want an ice cream, bro?'

'Why not?' Ank shrugs.

The order becomes three cones with flakes. All slurping ice cream, they head towards the play area and sit on a bench. Three County Lines operatives thoroughly enjoying their Mr Whippies.

They have a good couple of hours at the park. Joey wants to say, 'Let's go home and have some lunch.' That's what his mum would have said, but he knows there'll be no food at the flat and the people there will be busy cooking crack and loading drugs into bags belonging to older kids.

Instead, they call in at the Co-op on the way home and pick up meal deals, which they eat on the same bench that Billy sat on after he was stabbed. Candace makes no reference to that night, she must have been oblivious to what happened. Joey makes sure all the litter is placed in the bin and they head for flat 2.

'Do you like Ank?' Joey asks as they walk. 'He's taking you out tomorrow. I'm busy, I've got to go to work.'

Candace makes a concentrating face as she processes Joey's words. 'Are you coming back, though?'

Joey smiles. 'Yeah, Candy. I'll see you after work. But you make sure you have a fun day with Ank and be a good girl, yeah?'

She nods. Ank smiles, but when Candace turns away, the smile turns to a frown. His expression suggests that he's dreading spending the next day with a five-year-old girl. He's got to do Epping, Enfield and Harlow. It's a dry run for Ank with Candace. Billy wants to try out Epping to see how many clients they can get to by foot and bus in broad daylight. Ank's confident that the answer is a high number. But with Enfield and Harlow on top, it's going to be a long old day. He knows where he is in Epping, he tells Joey, but Enfield is not his patch, it's Ricky's. Joey knows this, too. It could be dangerous. Joey wishes it was him going with Candace tomorrow. He's not sure that Ank has the patience, or the interest, to look after her properly, especially if something kicks off. But, he reminds himself again, Candace is not his problem. He is not responsible for her.

At the flat, Joey says goodbye. One of the cooks makes a too-loud reference to *Sesame Street*. Joey catches it and ignores it.

Back at flat 1, there's a knock at the door. It's an older guy, Asian, with brown teeth. 'Is Joey around?'

Joey's about to ask who wants to know, before introducing himself, but the man says, 'You must be Joey's flatmate.' He goes on to describe how he's looking for someone more fitting Billy's description who answers to the name of Joey. Joey's about to put him straight then thinks better of it. So, Billy is pretending to be him? He'll have his reasons. The man explains that he's Arnav, the caretaker of the flats.

'I'm checking in with everyone on this level because I've had complaints about the flat below you. People coming and going. You seen anything?'

Joey smiles. 'No mate, I ain't seen anything or heard nuffin' at all. The flat below? That's Lorna and her little girl, yeah? They're as good as gold.'

The older man thanks him and goes on his way. Joey suspects that Billy must be flying under the radar and somehow bagged the flat through his probation officer, despite not using his own name. Joey decides to keep this conversation quiet. No need to alert Billy to the fact that Joey now knows how the land lies. The flat is in Joey's name, not Billy's. That's interesting. That means that Billy is using other people's identities to get homes. Joey knows there are people on waiting lists for years, so how does Billy do it? He shakes his head. Billy seems to have his finger in every pie there is.

XII

Candace

'Hello, Candy, ready for a day out?'

It's the man from yesterday, Joey's friend. Not that they seemed that friendly with each other.

'Where are we going?

'You have to tell me, or I'm not coming.'

Ank thinks for a minute. 'A place called Epping. Then Enfield. Then Harlow.'

'Do they have milkshakes there?'

Ank nods. 'Yep, yeah, they definitely do.' Candace isn't sure she believes him. His eyes dart about when he talks.

'Right, I've got your backpack. Pop it on.'

It slips off her shoulders. Whatever's in there isn't that heavy. Ank must have forgotten some of the things.

'Is my water bottle in there?'

'Er, no. D'ya need one?'

Candace nods, solemnly. 'Joey always packs me a water bottle. He says I have to drink because of all the traffic and walking.'

Ank finds the water bottle and fills it up, then they head

down the stairs towards the bus stop. It's a bus first, and then a train.

'I didn't have any breakfast,' Candace says, while they're waiting for the bus. 'I'm hungry.'

'Why didn't you have breakfast?' Ank sounds cross.

'Joey says I have to have breakfast when we're going to be doing lots of walking.'

'Joey says a lotta things.'

At first Ank chats to Candace, but when they are on the bus he looks at his phone.

'You're very busy,' Candace says, with a tone of accusation. 'Joey says it's rude to look at your phone all the time when you're with someone.'

'I got stuff to sort out,' Ank says. He doesn't look very happy. 'We're going to Enfield first.'

They get off the bus and walk quickly through the station to the train. Candace wants to go to the toilet. Ank says there isn't time. She says she's still hungry. Ank ignores her. As they walk, she holds her hand on her crotch to stop the wee coming out. Her bag slips off her shoulder and she can't carry it properly. She starts to cry. Ank doesn't notice. Or he doesn't care.

They're at Liverpool Street and they get the overground train to Enfield. Candace is crying harder now. On the train there's a group of primary school children in high-vis jackets with teachers and assistants also in high-vis. The children are excited and talk a lot. The grown-ups with them look nice. Candace watches the children with curiosity. Who are they? What are they doing? Are they at school? Is this what school looks like? The teachers are talking to each other and one of them points at Candace. Ank sees the teachers and grabs Candace. They jump off at White Hart Lane. It isn't their stop so they have to wait for the next train. Candace thinks Ank might be a bit stupid, getting off the train at the wrong stop.

When they get off the next train, Candace says that she really, really has to go to the toilet.

Ank is really cross now. He grabs her arm roughly and they go into a pub.

'Will you wait outside for me?' Candace asks.

'Yes, I'll be here. Just get on with it.'

Back on the path they follow Google Maps to the first block of flats.

'Don't you know where you're going?' Candace asks.

Ank tells her to shut up.

'That's not very nice. Joey doesn't say shut up. I'm going to tell Joey.'

'Jesus Christ, kid. Would you give it a rest?'

They find a place to stop, but there's no bench to sit on, so Candace sits on the ground while Ank takes all the little packets out of her backpack and gives them to ugly men in dirty coats. The men walk funny, and they scare Candace with their staring eyes, but there's no point telling Ank. Her leggings are wet from the damp ground and there's nothing to do.

She doesn't like it when one of the women walks up to her and starts to touch her face and hair.

'You're pretty, aren't you? Come on, come with me.'

Candace doesn't want to go and wrestles her off. The woman laughs and walks on. They finish business and move on to the next block and the next. Candace is very tired and she has a pain in her tummy. She is utterly miserable. She still hasn't eaten, but Ank won't listen. They do another block but haven't been anywhere near Epping yet. It's getting late and Ank doesn't have as big a pile of money as Joey gets.

'That's because Joey must work you harder than I have. Tomorrow we'll have to start earlier and you'll have to shut up.'

Candace doesn't like this talk of 'work'. She doesn't want to come tomorrow. She'll tell Joey. There's been no milkshake and no food. Candace cries again as they walk towards the bus stop.

'Shut up with your whingeing!' He shouts. 'My feet ache and my back aches, too. You're not the only one who's bloody well tired.'

When they sit down on the bus, Candace goes and sits in a separate seat, a long way from Ank.

As they near the flat, Ank seems anxious to get away. 'You don't need me to walk up the steps with you. I'll stand here at the bottom. You know your way, yeah?'

Candace nods. Of course she knows her way. But she is so tired. She climbs up the stairs, holding onto the rail as she goes, each step an effort. But, at the door of their flat, there's her mum's stuff outside, lying on the floor in piles. Amongst all the things is JoJo, her black whale that Joey bought her from the aquarium in Brighton. She reaches out to pick it up and, just as she does, a group of police run up the stairs behind her and another group comes from the other end of the balcony. Their feet pound on the balcony floor and echo around the estate.

She grabs her whale and sits near the top of the outside stairs. She puts her thumb into her mouth.

The police pile into her flat. She curls up against the wall to make herself small and watches as men are dragged out by the police. It's like watching a programme on TV. A couple of the men jump out of the toilet window and run past Candace, nearly pushing her over as they charge down the steps as if they're in a race. There is no sign of her mum.

But, suddenly, there is Joey. He is walking up the stairs. He sees Candace, sweeps her up, runs up the stairs to his flat and goes in. Billy is in there, sitting in the dark. Joey walks in and turns on the lights.

'Sshh,' Billy says and puts his finger to his lips.

Joey says nothing. He walks Candace to the kitchen. She is crying and her head is hot. Joey closes the kitchen door behind them, so Billy can't see when Joey gives her a big hug. She cries into his grey hoodie.

He squeezes her tight. 'It's all going to be okay.'

Finally, he asks her if she is hungry. She nods her head.

The freezer is full of chicken nuggets and frozen mashed potato. 'Good job Billy eats like a kid in care,' Joey mutters. Candace doesn't understand what that means, but Billy opens a can of beans and heats up the oven. He looks in the cupboard and pulls out cans of Pepsi Max.

'I wet myself,' Candace says, and lifts up her skirt. 'Twice.'

'Don't worry, Candy.' Joey lifts her up and carries her to his room where he pulls out a clean T-shirt. 'Come on.' He takes her to the bathroom and turns away so she can get undressed.

She stands on the slip mat in the shower and Joey washes her down, covering his eyes. He washes her clothes out in the sink and rolls them in a towel to wring them out, then hangs them on the back of the bathroom chair.

The T-shirt is like a big dress, but it is nice to be clean. Joey picks Candace up and carries her to his bed.

'TV?'

He turns it on and finds the Disney channel. He brings a drink and a ham sandwich. 'To keep you going till the nuggets are ready.'

She feels better with some food in her tummy. 'Is Mummy okay?'

Joey turns away. 'I think so.'

He doesn't sound sure. Candace doesn't know if the policemen have got her. Perhaps they can look after her. She can't eat all the nuggets when they come.

She drifts off to sleep. 'I love you, Joey,' she says.

XIII

Joey

Billy's frantically trying to sort things out. 'Fuckin' Ricky. It was him. He called the cops – trying to close down my kitchen.'

'How d'you know it was him?' Joey asks.

'Because he sent me a fuckin' text message asking me if I was enjoying the heat. Bastard. He must be running scared because we're doing so well. Threatening his business.'

Billy explains how he managed to get out real quick, as soon as he saw the first cop car and it was clear something was going down. He ran upstairs the long way round, from the other end of the balconies, to lose anyone who might have been following. He hid in the dark until Joey came in carrying Candace.

'It's been a shit day all round. Ank's fuckin' useless. He messaged me to say that Candace is a waste of space and a pain in the arse. All she does is cry and slow him down. He says he's gonna do the Epping run early in the morning, there's more hope for that delivery route because it's near some posh houses. He didn't come in, which is just as well.

He dropped Candace back to the flat, says he'll reload in the morning.'

By the time dawn comes around, Joey has a crick in his neck from spending an uncomfortable night on the sofa. Candace seems better though. He's left her in his room with a pile of snacks and told her to stay put until it's safe to come out. He catches one of the neighbours as he walks along the balcony toward the stairs.

'Did you hear that commotion last night? Gawden Bennet, that was mental!' the man says.

'Yeah, it was mad, wasn't it?' Joey agrees. 'Do you know what happened there?'

'Well, Lorna and her little girl have gone. God knows where. No one's seen 'em. The flat was raided by police – about a drug gang, apparently.'

Joey shakes his head. 'That's bad, real bad. Are the police still there?'

'Nah, they went hours ago. They arrested some and some got away. Arnav's trying to get in and tidy it up, but the police won't let him. The forensic team is coming.'

Joey tries to piece together what's happened. Where the fuck is Lorna?

He goes back to Billy. 'You got Lorna's number? I want to let her know that Candace is okay, just in case she's worried.'

Billy agrees to text her. *Lorna, where are you? Candy is here and safe. Joey is looking after her, the police won't let anyone in your flat.*

She messages back: *I'm at Shells on the next floor, say hi to Candy, Mummy loves her and tell her to eat her greens.*

'Eat her greens? That makes no sense. And who's Shell?'

Billy shrugs. 'Some other silly bitch. What a mess. It's only a matter of time until social come round to do a check. When the pigs have gone, get Lorna back in there, clean it up and make it look good. I want that kitchen back in action ASAP. I'll go talk to the dozy cow!'

It transpires that Lorna was out when the police burst in. She'd finally got herself up and taken the tartan trolley to the shops to get some food and bumped into an old mate from the salon, so she stopped and chatted for a bit. Her friend was concerned about her. When her friend asked about Candace, Lorna said, 'She's at school'. So at least one of Billy's plans was working. Then, when Lorna walked toward the flats she saw the police cars, looked up and realised it was her flat they were raiding, so she scampered off to the High Street for a few hours.

She gets her story straight with Billy and Joey, so that when the forensic team has gone and the caretaker meets Lorna at his office door, she holds onto Candace's hand and pretends to be confused.

'I went to see my mum in Essex for a few days. When I came back my flat had been broken into. They've made a right mess of it!'

Arnav has no reason not to believe her. Joey watches as the caretaker walks up the stairs with her and heads to her front door. Every sign at the flat is that she's been cuckooed. It's what the police said. Lorna plays her part well, bursting into tears. 'Look what they've done!'

Drawers are upturned, the fridge door is hanging off of its hinges, the floor is covered in rubbish. Everything is filthy. Joey appears at the door to ask if they're okay. The caretaker is busy trying to calm Lorna down and looks out of his depth.

'Look, don't worry,' Joey says to Arnav. 'I'll help her sort all this out. Lorna and Candace can stay upstairs with me until we get it all straight again.'

Candace dances and claps her hands. 'Yay! Let's stay with JoJo!'

Arnav looks relieved to have a problem taken care of, at least in the short term. He also offers to help clear up the mess. 'I've got plenty of bin bags and gloves.'

Joey gets Lorna and Candace settled upstairs, where Candace already seems to feel at home. True to his word, Arnav greets Joey at the front door half an hour later. The two men start clearing the mess into the bags. Piles of Domino's pizza boxes, at least 20 large fizzy drink bottles, mountains of sweet wrappers and crisp packets all get shovelled in. The place stinks to high heaven.

'I don't think it's safe for a kid to be here,' Arnav shakes his head. 'It's filthy.'

Joey is fully aware that Billy wants them back in as soon as possible, and he wants it to be ready for when the social workers come round which, given the police involvement, will be soon.

'We'll make it safe,' Joey says, with grim determination.

Joey does multiple runs down and back up the stairs, carrying at least two heavy bin bags at a time. Arnav grafts for a couple of hours, then gets a call to help a pensioner over in the other block. 'But we've broken the back of it. I'll be back in a while.'

While he's gone, Billy comes down to inspect.

'That carpet has to go. It smells of piss.'

Joey fetches his Stanley knife from the toolbox he keeps in his room and starts cutting into the carpet. They roll up patches of it. It's filthy, but not as bad as the stained, stinking underlay beneath it. That's ripped up too and thrown into bags. Joey is back up and down, throwing the bags into the big yellow skips that seem to live perpetually outside the caretaker's office. He smashes the shitty old sofa apart and gets rid of that, too. They fill buckets with bleach and wash the floors. Under the stinking underlay is some 1950s blue and white tiles that run throughout the flat.

'It looks alright, that,' Billy says. 'Retro.'

Protected beneath the underlay, the tiles come up all right.

'How do you know that Ricky won't be back with his little soldiers?' Joey asks, as they scrub.

Billy smiles. 'Oh, that won't be happening. Yeah, poor Ricky was in a nasty car accident on the M25.'

Joey looks at Billy and pretends to smile, but this news makes him feel sick. Billy really does have fingers everywhere if he can organise that sort of shit. He is not the man to cross. Ricky should have known better. Joey is reminded of just how much further down the chain he is in comparison to Billy.

Billy continues. 'This time I want the kitchen to run properly. Clean, hygienic, just the drugs. No fuckin' youngies and their shit. Nothing to mess it up. I want this place run like fuckin' GCHQ. No one comes up here, we play happy little families. I only want the cooks and only two this time. I'm bringing in a new pair. These two are older, quieter, real professionals, will keep their mouths shut.'

'Yes, boss.'

'Then, when we have this place looking lovely and social have done their little look-see, I'm moving in. I'm keeping a close eye on my little asset. Little Candy-girl is making me a lot of money. And her mum ain't so bad when she scrubs up.'

Joey is always a bit shocked by Billy's fearless optimism, as well as his ruthlessness. He doesn't care about anyone. It's all just business. He just wants his money and he always talks about it as if it's his show – when they all know that just isn't the case. He's senior in distribution, sure, but his bosses work in the city. They reinvest the money, moving it around and washing it through an art gallery in London and a couple of the capital's top restaurants. Then it makes its way to the traders, who also don't mind a bit of coke. And around and around it all goes, on the money-making drug machine. Little Candace will never see those men and women and it's quite likely she will not make it past her 16th birthday. Her mum definitely won't last. Smackheads rarely do.

Billy disappears down the stairs and off to the nearby hardware shop for some paint. By the time he returns with the cheapest tins of white paint and some rollers and brushes, Joey has more or less finished the deep bleach clean.

'What about furniture?' Joey asks.

Billy points to the ceiling. 'We'll shift some of the stuff up there down here.' Then he laughs. 'Don't worry. You can keep your bed.'

Arnav comes back and congratulates them on their progress. 'I really appreciate your help, Joey,' he says, though he's looking at Billy. Billy doesn't correct him.

Joey and Billy work on late into the night, painting the walls. Then they all crash upstairs. Joey gives his bed to Lorna and Candace and sleeps on the sofa again. Then, in the morning, Billy and Joey carry every stick of furniture downstairs, even the curtains. All apart from the ones in Joey's room. Lorna and Candace are very pleased with their newly-decorated and clean flat. Lorna places a selection of Billy's eclectic and stolen ornaments around the place, taking pride in arranging them.

'One day I'll get this lot properly valued,' Billy says. Joey knows he's a big fan of the *Antiques Roadshow* and likes to watch to see if he has anything worth money. He thinks he has some pieces from the Ming Dynasty that he stole from a house in Petersfield when he was up country delivering drugs 10 years ago.

'The house belonged to some rich couple. It was stuffed with old shit. They were out for the evening so I helped myself to whatever took me fancy.'

Billy liked their dog. 'Took him too, got bored of its whining, gave it to some nitties who lost it. Probably ended up at the RSPCA. It must have been chipped, they were proper people so they probably got him back again. Who knows? That's where I got this pot,' he says, pointing to a blue and white ginger jar.

'It's probably worth summink, so whatever you do, don't break it.'

On hearing that information, Lorna puts it on a high shelf. 'Away from your reach,' she says to Candace.

It strikes Joey that Lorna has no clue about the reaching capabilities of Candace. She's quite an agile little climber. He's seen her standing on the back of the sofa to pull back the curtains.

But the flat looks nice now. No question. It's been transformed. Billy's right, the floor looks retro-cool. To reduce some of the bleachy odour Joey has left open the small top windows and, for now, the front door. It doesn't look lived-in yet, and it doesn't look like the home of a five-year-old little girl. Billy must be thinking the same thing. He stands in the doorway, with his hand across the lower part of his face, moving his fingers to inspire ideas.

'What toys you got?' Joey asks Candace, but he already knows she doesn't have much. She brings out the black whale from her rucksack that she's got used to wearing all the time, like a tortoise. Then, from her room, she fetches the Stitch teddy, plus a sad old Barbie doll with sticking-up hair, and a couple of tattered old storybooks from a reading scheme that Joey recognises from his own childhood.

'Fit for the charity shop.'

'Nah, no good. We need this flat to look like a home,' Billy says. 'But that's given me an idea.'

The four of them head to the High Street. Where there was once a full range of different stores, now nearly all the shops are charity shops, barbers, nail bars or bookies. Billy has contacts in all these shops, except the charity shops.

Billy walks through the door of the first one and aims straight for the children's section. He grabs a pile of books and makes for the counter. Joey snatches them back.

'It's got to be believable. Candy is not into Ninjas.'

'Fuck's sake,' Billy mutters.

'Leave it to me,' Joey says, soothingly.

They leave with a dolls' house, new dresses, pink wellies, a little table and chairs, plastic teacups and plates, and a little plastic shop counter with a till and groceries. There are also teddies and dolls, books and posters for her room. In the last shop they even find a pink duvet set with Lilo and Stitch on it. It looks nearly new. Candace skips all the way home as the adults carry the hoard. There is a tonne of stuff. She's has never had this much stuff in her life.

Arnav sees them return and waves. When he comes over and sees all the purchases, his face breaks into a smile.

'This is wonderful. After something bad there is good!'

Candace is beyond happy.

Back at the flat, Joey is pleased to discover that the bleach-smell is much less strong. They put all the new stuff in the middle of the floor.

'It still feels a bit cold,' Joey says. 'That old tile floor needs a rug or two so she can play.'

No sooner has he said the words than the caretaker appears at the door with two rolled up rugs under his arm. Arnav waits at the door until Lorna invites him in, not wanting to intrude. He places them on the floor; one is still in the plastic it must have been bought in.

Arnav shrugs. 'People throw all sorts of things away. I keep a lot of stuff in the big store by my office.'

The rug in the plastic turns out to be a large circle of pink fluff. Candace lies on it and does a rug angel. Joey sees that even heartless Billy can't stop a grin from appearing on his face at her joy. The other rug is a plain gold rug, but it's a good size and covers much of the lounge floor. Having the rugs down makes the echoes in the flat disappear.

Candace sets up the little table and chairs in one corner and puts the teddies and dolls on the chairs, then lays out cups and saucers neatly on the table.

The caretaker looks at the scene. 'If one of you young

men doesn't mind coming downstairs to give me a hand, I have a little bookcase in the store that will take those books.'

Joey volunteers and returns shortly with an IKEA bookcase and a big basket to put the toys in. It's the little touches that really make a difference. Now the flat really does look lovely and welcoming. While Lorna and Candace are sorting out the rooms, Billy stands in the kitchen figuring out how to run it so that it can be returned to a proper kitchen at the end of each day.

'Maybe I get the cooks to work nights so no one can see 'em?'

Joey can almost see the cogs working in Billy's head.

'That's it. Night shifts.' But Billy isn't finished yet. He only ever wants more. 'We leave it as Lorna's kitchen in office hours, nine to five' he says. 'The social won't come outside their working day without good reason. We can work overnight and all weekend on production.'

Suddenly he claps his hands together. 'Right, this kitchen needs to look like a proper kitchen.' He gives Lorna a £50 note. 'Go to the shop and get fruit. I want it in bowls on display, looking healthy. I want the cupboard full of tins of food, and I want fresh veg in a veg rack.'

Lorna looks bewildered. 'We haven't got a veg rack.'

'Then get one. For the social. When they do their statutory visit, you're going to be polite and helpful and, more importantly, look like and *be* a fuckin' amazing mum.'

Lorna nods. 'Yes, Billy.'

'So you'll cut down the gear for a bit, yeah?'

'Yes, Billy.'

'What else?' He stands in the front door and looks onto all the other flats.

'Oh, yeah. Washing! You need washing on a line. Get pegs and a line. Joey'll put it up.' He hands her another £50. 'Get tea towels. Get all the fuckin' props, will you?'

'And a milkshake prop? Can I have a milkshake prop?' Candace asks.

Everyone laughs.

XIV

Candace

The sun shines through the window and lands on the clean white walls. Candace likes the way the light shows up the runs and drips and spills of paint in the walls. Everywhere is white. Even her room. You can see patches of the old wallpaper beneath it in some places, a reminder of their old life. She skips and hops from her room to the sitting room.

She likes it in this new, smarter version of their flat. The curtains are nicer, everything is brighter. It's also dreamy to have fruit, packets of cereal and a cupboard with jam and chocolate spread, fresh bread and all the little jars that her mum says are herbs and spices. There is even a jar of milkshake mix. Candace breathes in the smell of it all. The cupboard smells amazing. She opens the door of the fridge, just to look at it again. It's a great view inside there, too. Milk, cheese, strawberries, raspberries, proper butter and spread. There is bacon and ham in the clean meat drawer and salad vegetables in the big salad drawer at the bottom. It looks like the sort of fridge that people have on the television.

It makes her feel safe.

The washing machine has been washed too. It used to be all black around the edges but now it looks like it could actually get things clean. There is a safe tub on the side full of detergents and washing powder. This is something else that Candace had never seen in her home before.

Her mum is also behaving more like a mum. If their house was nice and tidy all the time, maybe she wouldn't need so much of her medicine.

Lorna stands like a waitress and uses a funny, posh voice when she says, 'Your ladyship, what would one like for breakfast?'

Candace hasn't seen her mum laughing and being funny since long before they met Billy. Candace points at the Coco Pops. Her mum does a theatrical hand movement and bows like the genie in *Aladdin*. 'Your wish is my command.'

Candace sits down at the table and looks around at all her new toys. While her mum gets the bowl and spoon out, Candace contemplates which toys to play with first. There are so many! Too much choice!

After breakfast, Lorna washes the dishes and puts things away, something else she never normally does. Candace runs to her room to put on one of her new dresses. She bounces back in, her hair wild where she has pulled the dress over her head.

Lorna laughs. 'Come here, monkey, I need to do your hair.'

Candace is only too happy to comply. It's nice feeling her mum play with her hair as Lorna tames the curls into a ponytail.

Then off she goes, straight back to her new play area and loses herself in a game of tea parties. Lorna collects the towels from the bathroom to put in the washing machine. The top windows in the whole flat are open again to let out any trace of bleach, and sun is everywhere, as if it's trying to make up for all the times of darkness in the flat.

Once the towels are done, Lorna pegs them outside on the back, private balcony where Joey has made a line. Candace is only too happy to help, even though it interrupts her game. The towels smell so nice. When they run out of room on the balcony, Lorna remembers an old clothes horse in the broom cupboard. Candace wonders why they never used it before. It's much better than the backs of chairs to dry things on.

They empty out the old laundry basket in Lorna's room and put another load on.

'I can't remember the last time I saw the bottom of this!' her mum laughs.

They put the next load in. The sound of the washing machine is loud but it has a nice rhythm.

The door goes.

'Is it JoJo?' Candace says.

'Or Billy,' her mum says.

It's neither of them. When Lorna opens the door,

outside are two women standing in the frame. They look smart. They have handbags over their arms.

'Hello, Lorna Murphy?'

Lorna nods.

'I'm Sarah Clayton and this is my colleague, Beth Anders. We're from child protection.'

Lorna sighs.

Candace is worried. These women can't take their nice, clean, new home away, can they?

Lorna invites them in. Candace doesn't like the way they look around at everything. They are very nosy. But it doesn't matter because their flat is nice now. Much better than it was before.

There is nothing to be nosy about. Candace returns to doing breakfast for her teddies and dollies. She looks up and smiles.

'You're busy, there,' the one called Beth, says.

'Would you like a cup of tea?' Candace says, holding out one of the cups and saucers of her new tea set.

Lorna laughs and invites them into the kitchen for a 'proper cuppa'. Sarah follows her through the door, but Beth wants to sit next to Candace and join in her play. Candace doesn't mind. It's always nice to have a friend to play with.

'Have you had any breakfast yet today, Candace?'

'Yes, I had pops and toast. Mummy said I can eat fruit, if I'm hungry, until it's lunchtime.' She points at the apples and bananas in the bowl on the table.

Sarah asks Lorna about school. 'Oh, she's on the waiting list,' Lorna says. 'Hopefully it won't be long.'

Candace overhears and is excited by that answer. A waiting list for school. Beth asks more questions.

'Have you been out recently? Have you been on any trips?'

Candace grabs her little black whale and holds it up. 'I went to the Sea Life centre and the beach and I got this! He's called JoJo.'

'That's lovely.'

'And we went to the park and the mu-see-umm.' Candace has to concentrate on saying that word. Joey taught her how to slow it down and sound it out.

Beth doesn't ask about Joey, so Candace doesn't tell her.

Sarah asks to have a look around the flat.

'Of course. Though you'll have to excuse the chaos,' Lorna says, gesturing to the washing hanging at the back. 'It's wash day.'

'Lovely drying day,' Sarah says. 'Nice breeze.'

'Hmmm,' Lorna agrees.

Her mum looks very tired again now. She seems to have stopped talking so much and smiling. It must be time for her to have some more medicine. So it's a good job that the ladies are leaving. They don't stay to drink their coffee that Lorna has made and put on the kitchen table, but they thank her anyway. Lorna sees them out, closes the door and watches them through the window as they walk along the balcony and disappear out of sight.

She high-fives Candace. 'Good girl, Candy-girl. You were very nice to the nosy ladies.'

Candace smiles and quickly gets back to her game.

XV

Billy

Billy lets himself into Lorna's flat. He's sorted out a key for himself so he can come and go as he pleases, as well as keys for the cooks.

His home, his proper home, isn't the flat upstairs that he's using with Joey, he actually has a smart warehouse conversion in East London, but the less people know about that, the better. He bought it as seen, but he's hardly there. It's not a home yet. It's more of an investment for the future. He goes there sometimes when he needs to escape. He likes a bit of quiet to recalibrate, but he is at his happiest when he's working. He prefers it here now, especially since most of the furniture went from the flat upstairs. He hasn't given Joey a key to Lorna's flat yet. He might not. He's not sure about Joey at the moment… his focus.

At least Joey does as he's told though, and that's the main thing.

The more he thinks about it, the more it feels like a bit of a waste, having that whole flat upstairs with only Joey in it. He wonders if there's a way to turn a bigger profit. Perhaps they could all bunk up down here running the kitchen most of the time – and run another kitchen upstairs 24/7. It's a thought. He might investigate that as an option. Billy clocks up the numbers in his head. With a second kitchen running he could do at least 500k a week. He doesn't need to, he has more than enough money with the first one, but he is addicted to the adrenaline rush, always looking for ways to grow the business – and there's always pressure to make more.

The kid is in the corner, playing. When he looks at Candace he can only see pound signs. He can get Candace out every day and night if she's not going to school. The social are off their backs for the time being. If she's tired she can sleep in. Most business happens after lunch anyway. Billy is a happy man. Ricky's raid has done him a favour in a funny sort of way.

He squeezes Lorna's arse – what there is of it. 'I'll be around here a bit more, babes, yeah. It's gonna be good.' He turns to face her in the kitchen, away from Candace, pulls up her T-shirt dress and sticks his two fingers straight into her vagina.

She giggles.

He wriggles about inside her, pulls his fingers out of her and gets her to suck them like a lolly. He pulls her dress top down and drags out her nipple. He starts tuning it like a radio. 'I'm feeling we should lie down.'

'Bathroom,' Lorna whispers. 'I can lock the door.'

He holds her arse as they walk past Candace.

'Yeah, I'm not sure what's wrong with the shower hose, Billy, perhaps you can take a look.'

She's become quite the little actress in the aftermath of the raid. He squeezes her right butt cheek hard, until she winces. 'I think the hose is a bit stiff,' he says, pushing her hands to feel his hard-on. 'Yeah, really very stiff indeed. It needs some fixing,' he says suggestively.

He locks the door behind them in the bathroom and pushes Lorna against the bath. She holds on tight while he lifts up her dress and pulls her knickers down to her ankles. He holds her hair tightly at the back of her head and grunts as he pushes into her. He lets go of her head and grips her shoulders pulling her harder onto him until he comes.

She groans, unconvincingly, too. But she likes it rough, he knows she does. Once he's composed himself, he slaps her on the arse and kisses her right cheek.

He pushes her forward roughly then goes again, this time in her anus. Lorna begins to scream – she isn't ready for this. He puts his hand over her mouth. 'Sssh. We don't want Candy to know her mum's a dirty bitch, do we?'

Lorna does as she's told, no longer resisting while he thrusts until he comes again. He walks backwards, tucking himself back into his clothes, unlocks the bathroom door and walks out without looking at her, while she scrabbles around for her clothes.

'Yeah, babe, a coffee would be great, cheers!' He calls.

Candace: The Gallery Girl

He walks to the sofa near Candace. 'All fixed now, Candy, the shower works great.'

'Thank you, Billy,' Candace says.

Billy nods with satisfaction. He owns Lorna's ass and her daughter is his slave. All is as it should be. Work is good. Life is good. He's already been out today, training up some youngies, teaching them the ropes while also putting the fear of God into them. He only needs to say 'Billy Bananas' and everyone complies.

Ricky's death in the car accident was never confirmed as murder but everyone knows that something would have made him crash. He never drove stoned or pissed, he was a professional who did his business and took it seriously. So it hasn't hurt Billy's reputation at all. The young kids know that he wouldn't think twice about dangling them over the edge of a building by their feet, or pushing them in front of traffic if they happen to breathe wrong in his direction.

You don't need urban myths when you're Billy Bananas. This is what he does and, just as importantly, what he is known for doing. He set a kid on fire and got away with it once. He knows everyone he needs to who can help him. He's connected to people in high places. He also loves a fight. He's always up for a good old scrap. He carries a blade and keeps a gun in his car, his very shiny BMW 5 Series. He thinks that a lot of his success is because he is way cleverer than anyone around him. He turns whole areas into his fiefdoms. And he's well on his way with this one. Ricky was a minor blip. Everything else is going to plan and when he's the unofficial King of London, he'll rule with an iron fist and fuck whoever he wants.

Billy can see that Joey is right about Candace. He's got a point there. They're better off looking after her properly. If she's in good condition, fed and watered properly, she will work longer and harder – and look the part. Her mum thinks she's Billy's wife now, so will do whatever he says. He's happy with that. For now. But there are other vulnerable single women across London with a young kid. Billy knows what he's looking for. He can spot these women a mile off. The same approach works every time and he wouldn't mind a bit more of a challenge. He thinks he might start hanging around in Clapham and Battersea with those yummy mummies. He'd love the pleasure of their resistance, but he knows that deep down, women like that, posh birds, as well as scum like Lorna, love a bit of rough. It could be fun.

But focusing on matters in hand, today is the last day that Candace will be enjoying her toys all day. Billy has plans for her to get back to work every day. He has heroin in his back pocket. He'll up Lorna's smack again now.

Joey walks by a little later, before he heads up stairs.

'Just checking in. Thought you might like to know how I got on today with the newest recruits.'

Joey also wants to check what his jobs are tomorrow. He waits for instructions. Billy is at the kitchen table wiping around his mouth, dabbing away the remnants of a stew that Lorna has made. Give her her due, she knew how to make an Irish stew. She doesn't have the accent, but her parents are Irish. He puts the crumpled square of kitchen roll on his plate where it soaks up the residual gravy.

'Right, Captain. I want you to go up by Fleet Street. A suited-and-booted will be waiting for you. He'll message you when you're close. There's a flattened bit of land near Deloitte's and there'll be construction workers nearby, so just wear a hi-vis jacket so you look like you're working on site. You can pick one up from that hardware shop in the High Street or nick our friendly caretaker's. Stand by Deloitte's looking at your phone. He'll be looking for you. There's a big party going off later. Media moguls, luvvies and the city kids wanting a snort or 10. I've already prepared you a bag.' He hands Joey a black cross-body manbag.

'This job is worth 20k. They pay double, this lot.' He smiles. 'They're too rich and stupid to even question it. Then I want you back 'ere asap. Those little kiddies on their scooters need you to direct them and be on the phones, yeah. I'm expecting another 20k from the blocks. There are 15 kids, yeah? You got all that?'

Joey nods.

Lorna clears his plate away, wipes the table and stands next to Billy. She leans on him and plays with the back of his hair.

'So that's probably time for you to fuck off, then,' Billy says to Joey.

Joey waves to Candace on the way out, who calls 'Night, Joey.'

XVI

Joey

Joey knows that the social were at the flat yesterday. Billy warned him before it happened. It's kind of weird that Billy knows everything. Like he's telepathic. He literally seems to know when things are going to happen. Most things, at least. Joey isn't sure that he knew that Ricky's boys were planning to fuck up the flat by calling the police. Maybe he did, in some perverted way, and let it happen as part of his plan. Who knows? Joey never knows what's going to happen next. He knows only two things: Candace is just a little kid who is caught up in something she shouldn't be, and he doesn't want to upset Bananas. The trouble is, those two things seem to be in contention with each other. He tries to avoid seeing Candace, but with Billy spending most of his time in flat 2 these days, that's hard.

And sometimes she's just *there*. This morning, for instance, as he was heading down to confirm a few things with Billy. There was Candace with her backpack on, walking along the balcony with Ank. She's back at work, then. Ank clearly has no idea about taking care of her, but what can Joey do? He can't say anything because he doesn't want to question the authority of King Billy.

He knocks on the door. Lorna is busy in the kitchen, burning a fry up.

'You're fuckin' useless,' Billy calls out to her.

At least Candace is out and can't hear Billy denigrate her mum.

As she goes back to the hob, Billy pulls out a wrap from his wallet. He holds it between his index and middle finger, and waves it up and down.

'I'm just trying to have my breakfast before she chases Mr Dragon, the fuckin' useless tart!'

Joey says nothing.

'Candace is back at work now the social have done their little look-see inspection. Back to business as usual.'

Joey pushes this, just lightly. 'Good that they came round. You was right, Billy. You know your stuff.'

Joey knows all about the size of Billy's ego. Even in prison, he puffed up with praise when it came to his wisdom and intelligence.

'I used to shag a boss in the social services, that's how.'

Joey pretends he isn't shocked and carries on chatting about the day, but Billy likes to boast.

'When I was 16, we were put in these assisted-living houses. The social rented them from landlords. Good fees, no questions. My landlord had smoke alarms in every room and hallway and they were always going off. Well, we were all stoned most of the time.' He smiles at the memory. 'The landlord complained, and this sexy, young, blonde social worker with tight jeans and long black boots shows up. Her name was Cat. She wanted to keep him quiet, so she took the batteries out the alarms. He never complained again and the neighbours couldn't grass us up. Oh yes, that Catherine, she was a *very* naughty gal.'

Joey turns his head. 'Lucky Lorna wasn't doing the cooking, or your 'ouse would have burnt down.'

Billy roars with laughter. 'She would come and check on us, to see if we was okay. Always up for a shag, mind. She was a dirty cow, she was. We all had her. Anyways, she's a big boss now and still up for a shag. She's the only woman I allow in my house, truth be told.'

That's news for Joey; he didn't know Billy had a house somewhere else. Joey carries on as though Billy has just talked about the weather.

Later, Joey stands leaning on the balcony watching for Ank to bring Candace back home. It's late, after 10pm, when he finally sees her little silhouette walking from the stairs below. She's on her own and her heavy legs drag along the balcony as though they are made of lead. He leans over to watch her get in through the door. It's still unlocked. Lorna must be tripping out still from the smack Billy cooked up for her after breakfast. He looks in the distance but can't see Ank. The fucker hasn't even walked her to the stairs. He let her come in, in the dark, by herself. What does he think he's doing?

He knows that if he gives an opinion on the subject, Billy

will be all over it. Joey would be moved away somewhere and he'd lose sight of Candace altogether. Joey pulls his own door shut, checking first that he has his key. He's in flip flops, tracksuit bottoms and a T-shirt. He realises that it looks like he's still in prison. In a way, it feels as if he is. He heads down the steps to Lorna's front door, noting that, in his head, it's become 'Lorna's front door' again, since the makeover. He opens it gently and sees the pink rucksack on its side on the floor. He hears Candace in the kitchen, banging about. She's trying to put some beans in a pan, struggling to pull back the ring lid on the can. He rushes over to help, worried that she'll cut herself.

'Hey Candy, you hungry, girl?'

She nods.

'Go and wash your hands. I'll cook your dinner.'

She goes obediently to the sink and uses her little step to climb up and reach for the soap. When she's finished rinsing them, she holds them up to him.

'Look, clean.'

Joey puts two slices of bread in the toaster and stirs the beans. He looks in the fridge to check there's plenty of cheddar.

'Cheesy beans?'

She nods enthusiastically and sits on the chair. He pulls open the kitchen drawer and puts a knife and fork on the table. He watches her tuck into the plate of beans on toast. She's very hungry. Her eyes are heavy and tired. After the food he helps her get ready for bed. She cleans her teeth and climbs up into her bed. Joey sits on the end of it, with a book, one of the ones they found in the charity shop. It's called *Beware of the Frog*. He starts reading, but by the time he gets to the first 'Gobble, gobble,' and looks up to see if Candace has enjoyed his silly voice, she's already spark out.

Joey tiptoes out, walking past Lorna, who is sitting in the armchair, her head tipped forward, her hair dangling across her face, her mouth fallen open.

It's a sad and sorry sight, but Joey feels somehow determined not to let it get him down. He makes sure everything is turned off and fills a big glass of water that he sets down beside Lorna for when she wakes. He puts the latch down on the door as he leaves and heads back up to his empty flat. The lack of furniture makes him think of prison again. He finds he doesn't mind that. A lot of this is like being in prison.

In the morning, a text from Billy arrives at 8am.

Morning darling, you up?

Joey replies: *Am now mate, you okay*

Billy reports that the kitchen crew are arriving today. *Can you see them in and set them up?*

Sure thing, Joey texts back.

Billy then phones with further instructions. 'Keep Lorna out the way, would ya? She had a big hit yesterday. I doubt she'll know what day of the week it is.'

'Righto.'

'Oh, and Candy is back out with Ank again today. The little bitch keeps complaining about the kid.'

'Why, what's up?' Joey asks.

'Ank doesn't like kids. Probably because he's a big fuckin' kid himself. He finds her a pain in the arse. But he has to keep her happy. The whole fuckin' point is that they go unnoticed and he's still walking round dressed like he's in the fuckin' Crips and Bloods from LA, when in actual fact he's a fuckin' low-life moron from the council estate.'

Joey doesn't comment. He wonders if he lets this play out a bit longer might he be back working with Candace. He doesn't want to look keen or offer help.

Billy uses Joey's lack of response to keep on moaning. More about Ank, then a few of the others, especially the ones who are under 18. Billy laughs cruelly about his latest recruit.

'Harry, from a very well-to-doooo family, you know,' he says, rounding out the vowels in a fake posh accent.

Billy loves getting kids from wealthy families, the professional families. It's like some kind of perverse victory when he gets one. Elsewhere he's recruited a GP's son and feels so happy about this little coup. He calls him 'Doc' and laughs every time he uses the nickname. Billy claims that the middle-class kids are a good target because they're given loads of stuff as compensation for busy parents. 'When they get to 17 they all get cars and that's when it gets exciting.'

Billy is creating a fleet of vehicles that he doesn't even have to fund the petrol for. 'Their parents pay for the insurance, MOTs, the lot.'

He has free drivers and cars galore. He chuckles again at his own ingenuity. 'It's so fuckin' easy. Too easy. All you need to do is keep 'em scared. The middle classes throw money at their kids. You know it. Therapists, camps, new toys. But what they don't understand, because they're privileged fuckin' morons, is that we've already got their precious kids. We have their minds, we own them.'

Joey thinks back to his own experience. All these years later he can see exactly how the gang brainwashed him, terrified him. He wanted to protect his mum. They said they'd rape and kill her if he didn't do as they said. They dismantle families like they're playing a game of KerPlunk, removing one stick at a time until the marbles fall through, each marble a child. Joey's mum once instilled good morals in him. He thought they'd all gone, but lately those morals have been knocking on his door. Despite being a convicted criminal, he never actively chose this path. He thought about going straight when he came out of prison, but there aren't that many great career options when you have a criminal record. While the gangs are just waiting there to pick you straight back up again.

But the way Billy talks, he's so dismissive of everyone around him. Joey can well see how Billy, and people like him, enjoy watching kids become victims of their power. It thrills them.

Joey is still struggling to process that a bosswoman in children services, if what Billy says is true, is in some ways as bad as Billy. This woman shagged minors, and it sounds as if she's still doing it. Man, the world is a fucked-up place.

How does anyone know who to trust? If he thinks back, trying to understand who is 'safe' in this world, it comes back to one person: his mum. He feels a bit like he's starting to wake up to what's what, rather than simply being dragged along by the filth of it all. He can begin to manoeuvre himself back to working with Candace. The only way to do that is by looking like that's the *last* thing he wants, because Billy loves it when anyone suffers or endures misery because of him. He is a disturbed man, a sick, dangerous man, born from a cycle of childhood abuses and unresolved issues of his own. Well, fuck him.

Late at night, after all his work is done and Candace is home, Joey has taken to spending his time drawing. He's set up some objects: a teapot, a jug and a bowl of fruit. He bought himself a A3 sketchbook from the post office. The shop was a shithole until recently, but it's got new owners and they've made big changes. They have art supplies that seem to sell out fast. Joey used to love art at school. He remembers his art teacher getting the class to do still life, hence the objects. And drawing was a way to pass the time in prison, though there he liked to sketch people. He loved all those subjects when he was young: art, music and drama. He wanted to go to art school at one point, but the gang made sure that never happened. County Lines is not interested in the arts – except as a means of washing money.

Imagine Billy being into the arts.

Joey can't.

When Joey sees Ank a few days later, he complains more about how Candace is slowing him down.

'She fucking moans all the time. She's a rat-girl from the sewer. Snivelling, crying, fucking whinging that she's hungry, thirsty, needs the fucking toilet or is tired. Fucking kid! What's wrong with her?'

Both Billy and Ank seem totally oblivious to the obvious fact that she's just a child. What Ank's just described: those are her basic needs. Why don't they see that? Joey knows the answer. To them, Candace is just a little slave. A robot who they'll dispose of when she is no longer any good to them. He knows it. He's heard Billy talking about it.

Billy has sat in front of Lorna when she is off her face on heroin, the heroin that he gives her to shut her up, and said, 'I'm going to fuck your daughter's arse so hard, I'll rip it in two.' Or, another time, 'I'm going to throw your whining little bitch of a child in the fuckin' river.'

Lorna just sits and stares at him like a zombie. She has no idea what he's said to her. She doesn't care either; she can't. Lately, Billy has started giving Lorna spice spliffs. Sometimes she sits, staring into space for hours, while her kitchen is busy with cooking and wrapping. Each day, Billy pushes it more and more. He originally said he wouldn't have the kitchen running all the time, but with Lorna off her tits most of the time and Candace out working, he's got it running nearly 24/7 on shift work again. He's brought in two other cooks from a different borough who go freelance for the best price. And all of it is taking its toll on Candace.

Joey returns to the flat and starts a new drawing.

He's started sticking his pictures up around the flat. He can see the improvement from picture to picture. He remembers listening to his art teacher's advice about light and shade, tone and perspectives. Drawing is helping him think and feel calm. He needs to think.

Suddenly there is a loud knock at the door. Through the spyhole, Joey sees that it's Ank, and he looks stricken.

'Ank, mate, what's up?'

'It's the kid. She's fuckin' dying.'

XVII

Joey

A film reel of horrible images runs through Joey's head. Billy and the blood after his stabbing. The gun Billy keeps in the glove compartment in his car. All the drugs that Candace carries every day in her backpack. Could she have ingested something? The traffic across London. The huge gap between the platform and the tube train at some of those underground stations. There are myriad ways that a child could be hurt.

'What do you mean?'

'She's lying on the floor, puking bad.'

Joey grabs his keys and runs downstairs, Ank a few steps behind him.

He holds back from appearing too concerned. If Billy sniffs out a weakness, he'll use it.

She really isn't well. She's pale and sweating. Neither Billy nor Ank know what to do when she vomits again on the floor in the lounge. They jump back from her as if she carries an electric charge.

'What the fuck is wrong with her, is she dying?' Ank says.

Billy says, 'Fuckin' hope not. It'll be a pain in the arse getting rid of a dead kid.'

Billy is already making a plan. 'If she dies we'll pack her up and put her in the river. Along with her mum.'

Joey hopes the fever she has is enough for Candace not to hear and register the coldness of Billy's words. County Lines isn't interested in health and safety, first aid or well-being. Slavery is free and the slaves are disposable. There's vomit everywhere. He looks at the two men. 'Let's get her off this floor. Put her on the sofa.'

Neither move. Ank's expression tells him that he doesn't want to go anywhere near Candace and Billy is scrolling through his phone.

Exasperated, Joey does it himself, laying her down flat and turning her into the recovery position, just as his mum taught him when he was probably only Candace's age.

He can hear her voice. 'Joe, if you youngsters learnt first aid at school, the NHS would save billions of pounds.'

Candace holds Joey's hand. Joey's eyes well up. He looks quickly at the men. Thank fuck they're facing the other way on their phones. He squeezes her hand and whispers, 'Shh, little one. You're going to be fine.'

'My head hurts. I feel horrible. I've been sick.'

Joey smiles. 'I can see that, Candy. It's fine. You'll be alright. I'm gonna get you some water. You need a drink. You're dehydrated.'

Candace's face relaxes, safe in the knowledge that finally someone is looking after her.

She doesn't look too bad. It's been a very hot day. Ank won't have taken a water bottle. She'll be dehydrated. Joey knows he needs to get some fluids inside her.

She begins to heave and is sick on the floor again.

'For fuck's sake, sort her out!' Billy calls as he retreats from the room.

Joey goes into the kitchen to find some kitchen roll and the mop. First, he needs to clean her face and put a cold cloth on her forehead and head to bring the heat down. Joey can't see her baseball cap. Perhaps she didn't wear it today. That would have helped keep the sun off her head. He glances in her room when he comes back with the water and sees it on the end of her bed. Sunstroke, then, maybe? He feels cross, but must not show any emotion about this, or fucked-up Billy will be all over it.

Joey walks back to Candace and gently sits her up, slowly encouraging her to take sips of cold water. As she does so, she looks into Joey's eyes. The trust he sees there almost breaks his heart.

Christ! Pull yourself together, Joey, he tells himself.

He's happy when she finishes the cup of water, and returns to the kitchen to fetch some more. With squares of damp kitchen roll, he gently wipes away the sick from her face and neck. He can help her to shower properly later, recovery is more important.

He scoops up the sick with the kitchen roll and soon amasses a pile of stinking sheets of it. He then gets the mop and puts a little bleach in the water in the bucket. He begins

Candace: The Gallery Girl

to clean. Lorna is in the armchair, shoved in the corner next to Candace's tea party table and chairs. She's been given spice again. She is paralysed, dribbling from the side of her mouth, oblivious. Joey makes sure that Candace doesn't see her. Her little head is facing the front door, not her mum. Candace doesn't even know she's there.

Billy marches back in and asks again what's wrong with her. 'I need her working, not fucking ill!'

Joey hides his thoughts. He stands up and scratches the back of his head with his flat palm. 'Ank, what did she eat today?'

Ank looks up from his phone. 'Err, I dunno, crisps?'

Joey pushes Ank but keeps his tone breezy. 'Yeah, is that it? Cos I'm thinking maybe food poisoning?'

Billy looks up. Joey knows he's watching.

'Naah, can't be. She didn't eat today,' Ank shakes his head.

Joey fakes a puffy laugh. 'That'll be it, then. I'll give her some more water and a bit of food. I'll keep an eye on her, yeah… she needs to be working. Are the jobs done for the day? I reckon I can sort her out so she can work in the morning, yeah?'

Ank pipes up, 'There's no fuckin' way I'm working with that fuckin' little moaning arsehole again.'

Joey plays it calm, plays it down. 'She should be fine tomorrow, Ank.'

He turns towards the sink to clean out the mop and bucket. 'Just remember to feed her,' he laughs.

He busies himself getting rid of the pile of vomit-covered kitchen roll. In the background, he hears Ank complaining.

'Look, Billy, 'ow many times 'ave I said I don't wanna work with a fuckin' kid? I can't do it. It's babysitting. I ain't working, bro, I'm making shit. She's slowing me down all the fuckin' time, man.'

Joey smiles to himself, remembering another of his mum's sayings.

'Slow and steady wins the race, Joe.'

He comes back out of the kitchen and says, 'Do you want her there, or shall I put her away?' He chooses his language carefully. As far as Billy's concerned, Candace is an object, just as much as the mop and bucket he's just put away. Joey needs to sound as if he believes the same thing.

He doesn't get an answer. 'Right, I'm off, then. Early start tomorrow; I'm driving to Weston-super-Mare.'

Billy is the one who told him to go to Weston-super-Mare. It's good operational business: 'There's a train station, it's off the M5 and there are boats in and out. You can zip to Devon, then out to Southern Ireland, good for drugs and trafficking, under the radar.'

Billy has been worming his way into that area for a long time. As with everything else he does, he smooths the passage because he's got contacts in the authorities. According to Billy, universities don't know how to do due diligence when it comes to recruitment of social work students. The unis are so keen to get the bums on seats, they haven't got a tick box for *Are you a County Lines elder using social work as a way of recruiting and controlling kids?* Money and fear rule the day.

'See ya.'

He leaves Candace on the sofa.

Billy calls Joey back, 'Ank, you do Weston tomorrow. Joey, you take Candace from now on.'

Joey makes a play of sighing and looking pissed off. He gives Ank a look as if to say, 'Are you serious? Thanks, mate.'

Ank offers a conciliatory shrug in return.

'Ladies, when you're ready, can you sort out your shit, and yeah, Joey, move the kid. I wanna watch a film.'

'Righto.'

Joey lifts Candace up and gently carries her to her room, where he takes off her dirty clothes and helps her pull on clean pyjamas. He gets two cups of water and leaves them by her bed. One might not be enough. She needs fluids. He puts a lamp down on the floor, so she has some light, but not too much. He picks up her rucksack and washes it off, leaving it to dry on the rear balcony.

Billy's voice barks in his direction. 'What are you doing?'

Joey explains that if he's got to go out with the kid tomorrow – and he makes it sound like a chore he doesn't want – he doesn't want to draw any suspicion towards them. 'A dirty kid always attracts attention. She's gotta look the part. No dirt, no moaning and crying.'

Billy nods. 'Turns out it wouldn't have been that bad if

she'd died. Looks like her birth was never registered. She could just disappear.'

Billy's words make Joey go cold. The man's an animal.

'Let me grab my stuff, then you can get off, yeah? I'll sleep here ready for the cooks, then I can load up in the morning.'

Billy seems pleased with Joey's initiative and is up and on his feet.

Joey is gone for less than 10 minutes and arrives back dressed in clean clothes. Billy looks him up and down.

'Yeah, you're definitely better at this. You look like a dad. Ank looks like a prick.' He laughs and walks out of the flat.

Joey sits down on the sofa and lets out a deep breath. He'd forgotten about Lorna. He shakes his head and wonders what the future holds for all of them. If there is one.

XVIII

Joey

By morning, Candace has made an almost full recovery. Joey checked in on her several times through the night. The cooks arrive early and Candace's rucksack is loaded up.

Joey doesn't need to speak with them. There's no point in small talk. They are focused and know their worth, so just do the job at hand and then wait to see if the money is right before they get a better deal. In the County Lines business, the cooks have become like chefs. The best ones have a degree in chemistry, or biology, or one of the sciences. They stick to the recipe unless otherwise instructed.

There's no sign of Billy today. He's busy elsewhere, on a different mission.

It's cloudy today, not the vibrant sun it was yesterday. Joey is pretty sure that Candace had sunstroke. It makes him hate Ank. He didn't like him anyway, but after the way he's treated Candace, Joey vows never to leave her alone with him again.

Unlike yesterday, Candace is wearing her cap over hair. Joey has done his best to tame the wild curls into a ponytail. She is wearing pink, knee-length shorts and a fresh T-shirt. He has rolled up a yellow raincoat that came from their charity shop visit. Joey sits Candace down on the sofa and brings her a bowl of cereal and a round of toast and jam. He makes sure he carries a bottle of water for her and one for himself. He also puts one of her picturebooks in her rucksack. He won't invite her to look at it on the bus, though, in case that makes her travel sick.

Candace is very happy this morning, happy to be going out with Joey.

'Do you want to say bye to Mummy?' he asks.

Candace puts her head down while holding his hand and says, quietly, 'No, thank you.'

Joey's drawing time has been productive in more than just the artistic output. He has been planning. Over the last few weeks and months he has gradually become more focussed on getting out of County Lines and all its connections. Seeing Candace in the centre of it all has really cleared his vision.

But that is hard to do.

You can't just walk away. There is no door marked 'exit'. Everyone knows that you either have to die, or leave the country. But in debt bondage you can't afford a night out, let alone an aeroplane ticket. He is patient. He watches. He keeps counsel with no one. He is quiet. He gets on with his work, always trying to make sure that he is not a

Candace: The Gallery Girl

problem, and doesn't get noticed. He will operate quietly and effectively. He always does what is asked, but not too much more, and never less.

As they walk through the High Street, he goes into Poundland. He doesn't want Candace to see what he's buying, so he asks her to choose some stickers from the stationery section. He picks up another pink rucksack, identical to the one Candace has on her back, but this one is folded and packaged and fits inside his own satchel.

Candace walks up with the stickers she's chosen. He pays for them separately and they leave the shop. Today they are back in the West End. Joey is doing Billy's route, because Billy rarely does deliveries anymore. He's concentrating on operations, and some new business venture that he's keeping quiet about. Joey is well aware of how he and Candace will look on camera, on CCTV. They look happy, as if they are father and daughter, having a fun day out. Candace skips along the path towards the train station. They do their jobs in the West End without any problem. No one gives them a second glance, they are effectively beige, despite the amount of pink that Candace enjoys wearing today. Joey is charging just a bit more to the clients. They're all minted and don't even seem to notice. Not much, just £20 per delivery. It soon amounts to £200 cash. He has all the right money for Billy, never a penny short.

Joey has been enjoying getting back into his art and wonders if Candace would like to see some art, too. They catch the underground to the Southbank and walk along to Tate Britain. Candace burbles excitedly about the boats on the Thames, the books laid out on tables, people everywhere and the strange, bright orange benches for sitting on.

She wants to sit on each one. Joey doesn't want to disrupt her fun, but is mindful that he is on a time schedule. They go into the Tate. Joey watches the amazement on Candace's face as she scans the huge space. Joey heads towards the Blavatnik Building, where there are lockers. He walks with Candace to the locker he's booked for a month, online. He pulls the new pink rucksack out of his man-bag and takes off the plastic wrapping. He opens it up, unzips it and puts it in the locker. He places the £200 in the bottom of the rucksack and locks the door again. Candace sees nothing. They head off back to the gallery.

There's a spring in his step. Joey feels excited about being close to art again. It's been a while. He remembers how happy it made him feel once.

He holds Candace's hand as they travel up the long escalator to the third floor, where the permanent exhibition is. They walk in, to stand straight in front of Picasso's *Three Dancers*. They stand to the side as a man in a straw hat, who looks vaguely familiar, maybe from TV, tells a younger woman about the painting. He is wafting his hand about as he speaks.

'You can see the way the three figures are angular and distorted, but he's captured them in a kind of frenzied dance. The whole effect is to reflect themes of love, sex and death, all of which are linked to personal tragedy in Picasso's life.'

The younger woman is lapping it all up, but so is Candace. She tilts her head to one side and points at the central figure in the painting.

'Look, I can see a turtle,' she says, loud enough for everyone to hear.

The famous man, whom Joey now thinks he recognises from the hours he's spent with Billy watching *Antiques Roadshow*, looks astonished.

'There's a dog!' she points to the orange shape in the middle to the right. 'Look, over here, there's a pink sausage dog with a big eye.'

The man looks at Candace and at Joey, as if he might be cross. Then the woman he was obviously trying to impress laughs delightedly. 'Yes, I can see them too!'

Candace's excitement is growing. 'I can see a monkey!'

People are beginning to gather around to take a closer look at the painting. The number one rule is that they don't draw attention to themselves. Joey tugs Candace's hand and quietly pulls her away. They walk out of the gallery on level three, heading toward the gift shop. Joey is amused and proud of Candace for undermining the pretentious description of Picasso's painting.

Joey's mum always used to say, 'Why does art have to be about sex? Why can't it be nice?'

Joey smiles as he thinks about Picasso having a laugh at

all the pompous critics by making a painting with hidden animals, or, if you are a bright child, like Candace, not-so-hidden animals.

In the shop he buys Candace a postcard of the Three Dancers along with a little drawing book and a pen. Why shouldn't she have a little memento of their day. They can't be controlled by Billy and his shag all the time. He also gets a new magnet for Candace to put on the fridge. That won't hurt to be in place in case the social pop back. Billy can't argue with that logic either.

Back on the road, they pass a newsagent by the pub and buy a couple of meal deals. Then they make their way back to one of the bright orange seats on the Southbank. Candace tucks into her ham and cheese sandwich and says, 'I like art, it's funny.'

'Shall we come back?'

Candace turns to look him in the eye. 'Yes, please, can we come back? I love it here!'

Another month passes. Joey wonders if he can have a day off. Or, at least, if Candace can. She's worn out. Even with the little detours and distractions he adds to their working day, she's exhausted. Most afternoons Joey has to carry her on his shoulders through London. He's fit, but his neck, shoulders and back hurt with the weight of her. He feels worn out. Billy works them all every day.

'No time off now, kiddies. No weakness,' he's fond of saying.

Which is fine for him when he's the one making all the

money. In real terms, Joey earns just enough to live on. He's been promised future promotions. He'll rise up the ranks and get a car. It won't be long before he's running an area of his own. Except that he knows he won't. He's not like Ank, who would cut your throat as soon as look at you. Joey isn't this and this isn't him. So he continues to bide his time, making sure that he keeps things tight at home. Food is simple and cheap. He doesn't go out. Everything is frugal. He feels like a monk in the monastery of Billy Bananas.

Joey is constantly worried about Candace, but if he expresses any concern Billy will see it as a sign of weakness and move in on him, so he keeps schtum.

Lorna is off her head all of the time now and seems to think she's Carmela Soprano, or something. She's complacent about all the criminal activity going on around her, because she believes she's a crucial part of the operation. How wrong could she be! She's nothing. She hasn't got a clue what's actually going on, and receives no financial reward, just physical abuse and drugs as and when Billy decides she can have some. Lorna only remains in her flat because that's useful to Billy: the kitchen, her daughter, her body – which comes gift-wrapped in a perverse eagerness to please. He knows when a woman has had an abusive childhood and he worms right into that pain to control them in a way that masquerades as care. They don't realise he's using them until he has them exactly where he wants them. Drugging them is just a means to an end. He enjoys drugging women. It gives him a sort of sadistic kick. The only reason Candace isn't drugged, or trafficked, is because she's currently a useful part of the Lorna takeover package.

The whole thing sickens him.

If Lorna is Carmela, that makes Billy Tony Soprano. He is like a mafia boss. Joey knows that there are eyes and ears everywhere. The whole organisation has people inside who will be working for Billy or some other gang. He needs Candace to be rescued from this and looked after. Time is running out. She should be in foster care, but with Billy's revelations about the former boss in social care, that avenue is closed.

Billy and his sex buddy at children's services have actually gone into business together, another one of Billy's little enterprises. Billy knows a very clever but dodgy accountant. He's in the process of organising the purchase of three large houses to use as private residential homes for kids in care. He's got a couple of other County Lines profiteers involved. They'll become shareholders in an investment portfolio of residential homes as part of a 'private equity wealth-management opportunity'. A great way for Billy to wash the money and shit on his own doorstep at the same time. The woman from children's services provides all the loopholes and makes sure the homes aren't set up as Ofsted-regulated institutions; instead they're unregulated homes. Although she has buried her name deep in the paperwork via other companies so that it probably couldn't be traced or proved. This means that they can do what the hell they want and cover it up. Billy will have access to all the children he wants. She knows exactly what to do to make sure it all goes beneath the radar. Billy boasts about it all the time. It's sickening.

Perhaps that's the catalyst for the day Joey decides to contact Crimestoppers. It's been a gradual build-up over time, a feeling that he must do something. They are independent and things can be reported anonymously. If he's careful, it can't come back to him.

He sits down by the window on his phone, so that he'll have plenty of warning to stop what he's doing if he sees Billy coming. On the Crimestoppers website he begins to complete a form. He gives enough detail for the police to investigate, but not too much to reveal himself. He offers the address, the set-up. He says that there are firearms and knives in the flat, because when the cooks work they bring guns for protection. Why wouldn't they? They earn a fortune and don't want trouble landing on them. He says that there's a vulnerable child, a girl, and her vulnerable mother is being cuckooed by a gang. He can't bring himself to use Billy's name. Not least because if there is someone dodgy in the chain and they see it, word will get straight back to Billy.

No one understands the IT capabilities of County Lines and its breadth of operation. Joey is under no illusion that he is anything more than just a tiny, disposable cog in the machine. The kids and their elders, who started out as little kids themselves, are all disposable – because Billy and his kind made sure their families broke down and gave up on their kids. Just like his family did.

He presses send.

XIX

Joey

No matter how tired they both are, Joey can't be seen to be the one suggesting that Candace doesn't work for a day or two. He takes Candace out on Sunday, where they do a few drops in Shoreditch. It's become a trendy area to hang out and be seen in. There are lots of well-paid media and arty types there and they love drugs like ketamine and coke, MDMA for the weekends. They like the thrill. They also love to drink. Joey wonders how they pay their rent. A glass of wine in Shoreditch costs more than he spends on four meals. It seems crazy.

Joey leaves Candace sitting on a bench, away from the gathering of young professionals who are too stupid to question what's in their 'designer' drugs. One of them died of an overdose a few weeks back because they used a dodgy supplier. The police wrote it off. Their parents might set up a charity to raise awareness if they can be bothered. Some of the punters are actually journalists, probably writing about the drug problem in London and across the country, who drop their morals for a snort or two of cocaine.

That's how it works: fucked up, broken morals. Broken everything. A stasis which allows Billy, and those like him, to keep raking it in and laughing all the way, because their empires are so easy to create from the combination of addiction, fear and messed-up middle class values. Poor kids can't afford these kinds of drugs. They have the shit heroin and crack, end up sleeping in doorways and disused buildings – but they aren't written about.

Joey looks around him, constantly, keeping one eye on Candace, who is yawning. Joey looks up at the old warehouse buildings and houses. They smack of Victorian London and he wonders how much has really changed since Charles Dickens wrote his books. Not much.

Joey is fuelled by his determination to leave and asks for 15% over the Billy-asking price. He walks away with £400 for himself. He puts the money in Candace's backpack, zips it up and walks off to Tate Modern, where they've taken to going some afternoons to give themselves a bit of a break. He heads over to the locker and takes out the extra money to add it to the rest in the other pink backpack.

They walk around and look at the art. It's become a haven for them. Candace loves being here for the same reasons he does: the scale of the building itself, the size of some of the art, favourite pieces that they are drawn to over and over again. Candace absolutely loves the shop, too.

Joey is feeling it today. Sometimes the futility of it all gets to him. His body is tired. He aches all over his neck and back and isn't sure if he can carry Candace today. They both walk slowly. He has a sense that he is being followed, someone – or something – has their eyes on them. It's a peculiar sixth sense, but he can't shake it off.

He takes Candace into the Tate Modern café. They buy a light lunch and drinks. It's a busy Sunday, the front and side doors are open, but he finds a seat that's by the wall between the two open doors. One faces Blackfriars, where there's a luggage storage place called Stashy's. A new plan forms. He's certain that the Tate is no longer safe. He can transfer the money backpack to there; start again. It's a shame, because the art gallery was the perfect cover, but the feeling of being watched won't go away and it has made every nerve in his body switch to high alert. There is over 3k in the hidden backpack now, enough to leave and start a new life. He doesn't want to jeopardise it.

Survivor mode kicks in. He settles Candace at a table, takes her bag and slings it over his shoulder. He orders her food and a soft drink. While she's tucking in, he goes back to the locker and retrieves the money.

'Good chow?'

She nods, still chewing.

He sits back down with his back against the wall, eyes everywhere. Hanging from a chair next to him is a mustard-coloured baseball cap. It belongs to a group of Italian tourists. He'll grab that on the way out. Candace has a pink cap in her bag. He sits with her bag between his knees, taking no chances. He rummages in Candace's bag and pulls out her cap and puts it into the manbag across his body. They eat their lunch and he makes conversation with Candace to keep it looking natural, to avoid alerting her to the fact that anything is different, and to help him keep his head.

He sees, out of the corner of his eye, two men come in. They look shifty. They don't look like they're here for the art. He was right about them being followed. His instinct is good.

Suddenly, one of the girls in the Italian group lets out a high-pitched scream as one of the guys pulls her onto his lap. It's a split-second, but it's enough.

'Get off!'

Everyone looks at the commotion, including the two men. It couldn't have come at a more perfect moment for Joey.

He stands, grabs Candace by the hand, swipes the mustard cap and is out of the side door in one quick move. He puts the pink rucksack on Candace back to front, so the bag is at the front and you can't see it from behind her. He gives her the pink cap and rapidly puts on the mustard cap himself. He removes his grey jacket. It's lightweight, so he stuffs it inside her rucksack.

He is calculating all the time.

He is also praying that they get away with this. He doesn't run. Instead, he walks casually, weaving through groups of people, calming screening them both with crowds, even though his heart is pounding. He slips into a newsagent and slowly, deliberately, chooses some sweets. There is no need to panic.

They sit on a bench, pootle around for a bit and, after 45 minutes, they walk in the direction of Stashy's, past the OXO tower, past Gabriel's Wharf. They take their time, slowly looking around to give the men even more time to give up.

When they eventually reach the luggage stasher's unit, he's certain he's shaken them off. He puts the mustard cap in the cash rucksack, thinking that it might be useful again at some point in the future. He'll also keep the money here for now. He can come back between the hours of 10am and 5pm. That gives him time during the day and at weekends to keep filling it.

They revert back to what they were wearing before.

The right cash is in the rucksack for Billy, and everything is fine, he tells himself.

Candace is none the wiser. She's had a nice day out, enjoying the art and the sights of London.

He can breathe again.

When they return to the flat, the cooks are busy clearing up and putting their stuff away in their box. They keep one big plastic container in the kitchen that's full of materials and equipment for cooking. The rest goes with them. They always take their base materials with them, never leaving anything incriminating behind. No trace. They always wear gloves and hardly speak. They are discreet and professional, and disappear back to the suburbs with barely a nod of acknowledgement to Joey.

Candace throws herself onto the sofa and lies down facing the TV.

Joey walks over and turns it on for her. When the cooks leave, Joey looks for Lorna. She's lying on her bed. The strap is still around her arm and Joey can see that Billy has been in to have his fill. Joey takes the strap off her, puts her into recovery position and pulls the sheet over her for some dignity. He pulls the door to.

'Are you hungry?' he calls out to Candace.

'Yeah, beeeans please!'

Joey smiles at her easy familiarity with him. He likes their little routines.

'Cheesy beans, or plain?' he calls back.

He hears a loud, 'Cheeeeeesy!'

He smiles again and gets to it. The cooks leave the kitchen spotless. They are very careful but still Joey takes no chances. He anti-bacs all the surfaces and the cutting board which they don't even use. With each passing day Joey feels more galvanised. He'll be gone. He'll leave this hell. So far he hasn't had any indication that children's social care are coming to visit Candace, or that his SOS to Crimestoppers has had any impact. But Candace needs to be in care to be safe and her mum *definitely* needs help.

Today was a warning though. Time *is* running out.

XX

Joey

By the end of July, the schools have broken up for summer and the weather is shit. Joey looks out of the window at the rain lashing against the glass.

Candace has missed an entire year of school. It's not so hard to see how she's slipped through the net. He's heard the whole story now from Lorna, in an all-too-brief lucid moment one morning. When Lorna and Reg, Candace's father, were in their tiny flat and Lorna gave birth, they were so disorganised they didn't even realise that Lorna was in labour. The baby was born at home. No one registered baby Candace's birth. Reg had seen a film posted on online that talked about how, if you don't register a baby's birth it will stop them becoming part of the authoritative corporation, or something like that. Lorna couldn't quite remember. It sounded to Joey like a good excuse not to go down to the register office, when neither of them could be bothered. Candace might be six now. She doesn't know when her birthday is. She thinks it's in the summer, though. Reg sounds like a total stoner and he didn't stick around long, so Candace has always lived in chaos. Joey has no idea how Lorna has managed to hang onto Candace for all these years.

The rain continues to fall.

Joey remembers his mum saying, 'Of course it's raining now it's school holiday. You kids will be bored stiff.' She would put him in holiday clubs, all sorts of things. He did sports clubs, arts clubs, scouts and camping, loads of stuff. As a nurse and a single parent, it would cost his mum nearly all her wages to put him in the clubs, but she always said she didn't want him getting up to mischief, wandering the streets when school was out. She got that wrong. County Lines was being introduced at school. Joey, like so many of his fellow pupils, felt unsafe at school. The teachers didn't know what was going on. They only see so much and, since so many of the schools became academies, reputations are built on academic results and behavioural reputation. The best way to deal with behaviour, if you are in denial, is zero tolerance – which equates to silent schools, where students are discouraged from speaking, even in the corridors. So, when Joey started to struggle and disrupt lessons in Year 8, because he was being groomed, and his mum asked for help, the school chucked him out.

Even though he'd never been in any kind of trouble before that.

The gang performed the oldest trick in the book and his school still didn't get it. Take a kid on the way to school, drive them around in a car filled with nitties who smoke

Candace: The Gallery Girl

weed, get the kid stoned and stinking of weed, send them back into school: kid gets excluded. As Billy would say, 'It's so fuckin' easy.' Joey felt used, but he never showed it. If anything, he presented himself as almost pathetically grateful to the gang.

Not any more.

He shakes his head and tunes back into the present moment, and the rain. He gets himself ready for the day and goes to get Candace. He opens Lorna's front door and sees a couple of letters on the floor. One is in a recycled paper envelope, the same grey as the letter he saw last time from the social. The other is a Saga Holidays flyer, probably intended for whoever the last occupant of the flat was. The cooks aren't here yet, so Joey steams open the letter. He pulls out the thick, recycled grey paper with the borough authority's logo at the top.

Dear Lorna,

We would like to visit you and Candace on 6th August at your home…

Joey smiles. This could be it. Finally, they can wake up and see that Candace needs to go into care. He puts the letter back in its envelope, sticks it back down and puts it on the side. He is always paranoid that Billy will suss something. He's like an alleycat with a PhD in mind games. He puts the letter under the flyer, under a newspaper that Billy has left. He loves reading the local paper.

He hears the door opening and in come the cooks. They are as silent as always, apart from a raised hand to indicate hello. They put on their gloves and forensic suits and set about organising their materials.

Joey thinks they look like members of the cast of *Silent Witness*. He finds their uptightness amusing and can't imagine ever wanting to spend social time with them. As they continue to busy themselves with the set up, he pulls down the cereal box and puts on some toast. There's no need for Candace to go out with her little tartan trolley these days; Billy has taken to getting Lorna's groceries delivered by Tesco. There's a steady supply of food. Billy can choose what they get in, and that way make sure Lorna doesn't go outside.

He considers her to be a total liability.

To avoid the possibility of her talking to people, he effectively keeps her locked up in the flat. He gets the same order every week, which explains why there are so many bottles of shampoo in the bathroom. In spite of all his money, Billy is a tight arse. He only buys the very basics. Lorna cooks him dinner a couple of nights a week when she can. Billy decides when and what, and makes sure that he controls her dosages, so that she'll be capable of doing what he wants. He plans for everything with the drugs he gives her. He likes to finish dinner off with sex. She is his puppet. Lorna never questions where he is the rest of the time, because he makes sure that she's out of it – off her face. There can be no questions then. Joey knows Billy has more than a few women in similar situations that he sees throughout the week.

Candace: The Gallery Girl

Joey ponders the different possibilities for the 6th of August. The various permutations of how it might play out. If no one else knows about the letter, then the social workers will walk into a trap house. They will be plunged into sight of the cooks making crack. They'll probably see Lorna off her face and, in all likelihood, no Candace. That won't work. Candace should be here, or they'll put a search out for her and that would mess up his own escape plans. Billy won't let Candace stay here when she should be working and those two cook freaks would tell him if he left her here for the day.

Joey keeps thinking. There must be an answer.

'JoJo, I'm hungry!'

In comes Candace, with crazy bed-hair. He smiles at her, but says, so the two snake cooks who hear everything can report to Billy, 'Good, good. You need to eat plenty so you've got the energy for today's jobs.'

Billy has already sent Joey the day's list first thing. He takes the orders via a secure messaging app, where all the deals are done. It's up to Joey to order them in a way that works. Joey has already made a plan for today. He's pretty much like a London cab driver, in the sense that he has a detailed map inside his head, can work out the best routes and knows his way around London like the proverbial back of his hand. He ends with the nittie deals, the crack addicts who are the bread and butter of Billy's business. It's funny how it works. If they are poor, Billy gets them addicted as soon as he can – because they'll beg, steal, borrow or sell their own organs for a hit. The middle classes and the super-rich, on the other hand, he needs them to be only recreational users. They have to be able to function and work to keep bringing him their money.

Joey plans his day starting with where the big money is, because he can zip to the luggage storage place and move some money into the other rucksack on his way to Tower Hamlets and Hackney, to finish the day on the nittie run.

He still can't shake the feeling that he's being followed. The day at the Tate, he's almost certain about, but he has no solid idea about who the men were or why they'd follow him. He can't mention it to Billy, in case it's Billy who's checking him out. If it's nothing to do with Billy, then he doesn't want to scare the horses. You make plenty of enemies in this game. He can't trust anyone, he'd be a fool to even try. He just needs to stay calm and be careful, leaving nothing to chance.

He doesn't want to cause any suspicion about tampering with the letter, so he decides to leave it where it is for now, disappearing under a rising pile of new, unopened letters.

'Come on Candace, time to go.'

He helps her put on her rucksack, prepared by the cooks according to the orders. Candace, breakfast now finished, yawns and stretches. 'What are we doing today, JoJo?'

'If you're a good girl out and about today, maybe I'll take you to a museum.'

This gets a raised eyebrow from one of the cooks, but in an approving way. Weirdly, the over-professional,

Candace: The Gallery Girl

middle-class cooks seem to think that's a sound plan for a girl who will have just, unwittingly, helped to deliver hundreds of pounds worth of drugs across the nation's capital.

Joey can't help but think, once again, what a morally fucked-up world County Lines inhabits. Everything is a double standard. The big bosses wouldn't let their own kids near the drugs but are happy to use other people's.

Joey has been doing a lot of thinking about all of this of late.

County Lines is not only the most capitalistic business model out there, it's also totally about class and status. It's like the American Dream, it places enormous value on wealth and the idea of being 'self-made.' Status is totally dependent on wealth, regardless of how that wealth was made. Financial success can be achieved through a person's own hard work, talent and determination, regardless of their background. The idea of the self-made individual is attractive, and deeply ingrained in American culture, but Joey knows that the reality is far more nuanced. Privilege and systemic advantages play their role. Joey felt poor as a kid. He sees now what little chance he had in a system that was designed to swallow him up. There really is no 'social impact policy' for County Lines.

Joey and Candace walk to the bus stop. Joey is wary and hyper-observant the whole way. They get the bus to the train station. They go back to a familiar haunt, to Ladbroke Grove, starting with the flamboyant man,

Colin, with the fluffy, white cats. He's nice and he's kind to Candace. She knows their routes by now and recognises the locations.

'Cotton's house,' she says, happily.

It's Colin's house, rather than the cat's, but Candace is all about the animals. 'That's right.'

They knock on the door. While they wait for Colin to answer, a blue BMW appears in Joey's line of vision. It looks out of place and catches Joey's eye. It's not the version of a BMW that would belong to someone living in this area. Here they're all either vintage or top of the range. This one looks like it was purchased from a dodgy ad on Facebook. Inside are two silhouettes, hoods up. The two characters in the Tate café were wearing hoodies, but they were down. Stands to reason. If they had them up in a place like that security would be all over them.

The cheerful antiques dealer and interior designer opens the door and welcomes them in. 'How are you enjoying your school holidays, Candace, love?' Candace looks at Joey, whose heart sinks at the question. Her answer could easily reveal that she is in fact a slave mule and that he is an evil fucker for being complicit.

Candace just shrugs her shoulders. The moment passes.

'You want to see Cotton? Of course you do. She's outside.'

The doors are already open. The man gets a soda from the fridge and pours a packet of Waitrose crisps into a bowl to take out to Candace, who is already sitting on the step with Cotton. Joey likes this man. He's kind and doesn't seem to know much about the drug world, beyond keeping his own customers happy.

'Another event for your customers?' Joey asks.

'Yes, it is. This time the Americans. They love to party. New Yorkers. A bit too connected to Trump for my liking, if you know what I mean; that world you know, Epstein and all that, but they pay me and my designers an absolute fortune to do their homes and holiday retreats, so I mustn't grumble. It is what it is.'

Joey decides that he likes this man less. The world around drug use is as corrupt as hell.

Joey then reminds himself that, for now, he must also be corrupt and overcharge him on this deal. And he needs to get the difference into the duplicate pink rucksack asap. And he needs to do it without those two in the BMW knowing.

Joey conducts his business, then goes outside to see Candace and the cats. The man follows him outside.

Joey is taken aback. 'Wow, what a stunning garden. It goes back a *long* way. I thought it was only to this bit.' Joey indicates the square that can be seen from the bifold doors, then gestures to the expanse beyond.

'Isn't it? I actually bought the house for the garden. It's the longest in the street. It borders the alleyway to the shops. I use the back passage, as it were, to get to the deli and florist. Very handy indeed.'

An idea strikes Joey immediately, but he plays a longer

game for a few minutes, carrying on the conversation, admiring the planting.

Then he turns to look at the back of the house, and the seating by the bi-folding doors. 'This has gotta be one of the nicest houses I've been in. You have incredible taste.'

Antiques Colin blushes, possibly because he quietly fancies Joey. Joey has picked up on this before and told himself, in the nicest possible way, never to come here without Candace.

'Is it okay if we use your passageway to the shops? We're heading that way ourselves.'

'Of course, be my guest,' he purrs, and walks them to the locked back gate.

That makes it easy to slip the two men and get to Stashy's to put the money in the other rucksack. Billy will know his delivery list, and that's not a problem as Joey has nothing to hide at Tower Hamlets and Hackney. As they walk back through Islington he looks in a café window and sees the BMW in the reflection of the glass and smiles to himself. They've caught up with him, because he's exactly where he's supposed to be at the right time. They've missed everything in between, and his stash is safe.

'Amateurs,' he mutters.

He enjoys getting the bus all the way back, just so they have the stress of trying to follow through the traffic, knowing he's got nothing for them.

When he and Candace get back to the flat, Billy is there.

Joey automatically feels guilty and on edge, and tries to read Billy's face. Only one of the cooks is there.

'There's a fuckin' surveillance van outside, at the bottom far end of the car park,' Billy says.

Joey moves to the kitchen window and looks out while filling the kettle, in an obvious way, so that his behaviour looks normal. He sees a conspicuous, bright-green Iveco van, with some sort of top box on it.

'The green one?'

Billy says, 'Yeah, I've been watching them today. It arrived a couple of hours ago. Cooks are leaving separately and wearing Lorna's clothes.'

Joey raises his eyebrows. He'd love to have seen that uptight male cook leave in a dress. He hides his personal thoughts and gets operational. 'How do we play it?'

Billy plays with his beard, then says, 'I'll get the kids out to disrupt it. Two days. We can manage for two days.'

'Righto.'

'You can't leave here until it's dark, so make yourself useful and make dinner.'

Joey smiles but feels like punching Billy.

Joey looks at the remaining cook, a woman who looks like a teacher. 'You want some dinner?'

She shakes her head.

He heads to the cupboards and pulls out tins of kidney beans and vegetables. He thinks he'll try to cook a rice dish. Candace likes rice.

'Oy, hang on a minute, don't cook any fuckin' Jamaican

shit. No spices, just plain food. Are there any nuggets in the freezer?'

Joey puts the ingredients away and pulls out the big bag of potatoes. He takes out a full packet of chicken nuggets and two cans of baked beans from the cupboard. He puts the oven on to heat up, then opens the bag and hands over the money to Billy.

Billy counts it twice and nods, 'Good work, kids.'

Joey is never sure if this is real, or sarcasm, or a trap. Billy's too hard to figure out. So he plays it down and avoids responding, hoping that way Billy will never suspect anything of him. The oven needs a few more minutes to heat up, so Joey goes to check on Lorna. She is more and more invisible these days. No one takes any notice of her, not even Candace. Everything that goes on in the flat just plays out around her.

She's sitting in the armchair in the corner. He walks up to her and touches her arm. She slowly turns her head to look up at Joey.

'Are you hungry, Lorna? Do you want some dinner?'

Billy walks over with his phone in his hand, looking at her as if she's a lampshade, deciding if he wants to turn her on after dinner or not.

Billy looks at her and then towards Joey. 'Yeah, give her some food. She needs energy for laters.' He makes a little clicking sound with his mouth to match his wink.

Joey goes into the kitchen and shakes out all the nuggets from the bag. He puts them on a baking tray. Then he speed-peels a whole bag of potatoes and cooks them in the bottom of the two-tier steamer, the bit where the water goes. There's not a pan big enough. Joey found this one in a charity shop and bought it because he thought it would be a good prop for when social come around, so it looks like Lorna steams vegetables for Candace.

The cook's phone buzzes. She says, 'That's me. He's waiting in the car.'

She's wearing one of Lorna's hoodies and pulls it up and down over her face, then puts the last of the incriminating materials in a shopping bag. Joey watches her go. As she exits the house, she bends down lower than the balcony wall, so that she's out of view of anyone watching from the van. She goes down the stairs like this, onto the next balcony, then pretends she's dropped something when a man walks by. She stands up when she reaches the other end of the balcony and turns to make it look as if she's come from the other direction. She walks all the way along the balcony below and down the final set of stairs, through the car park and onto the road where the other cook is waiting in their silver Tesla.

'That's her husband,' Billy says, with a chuckle. 'A right old pair, they are.'

Aren't they just, thinks Joey. He wonders if they have kids of their own. They're old enough to have grown up kids. How do people like that end up in a game like this?

Joey lays the table and calls Billy and Candace just before he serves up. He looks at Lorna, decides she isn't capable of making it over to the table, and asks if she wants her dinner on a tray.

She just stares into space.

The others sit down at the table, like they're part of some strange social experiment. Billy tells Candace to go get the ketchup. She jumps down to do as she's asked.

'What did you do today?' Billy asks Candace. Perhaps sitting at the table has reminded him about social norms. Joey has a mild panic about what Candace might say, but the reality is that she knows nothing. Hopefully her truth will match the truth according to the delivery list. He needn't have worried. Candace is tired, she doesn't like Billy and probably can't remember anyway, so she just shrugs as if Billy had asked her what she'd done at school today.

Like most kids who are asked that question, the answering shrug implies that 'nothing' was what she did.

Billy is smart enough to be watching Joey's reaction, so Joey asks, 'Are you tired, Candy?'

She nods. She looks like she could fall asleep at the table.

Billy stretches his arms like a peacock spreading its tail. He takes the ketchup and squirts it all over his chicken nuggets. Joey thinks he eats like a kid with no manners. Perhaps he never had anyone to teach him any. He stuffs the food in his mouth and most of it is gone before Joey has even had time to take the tray of food over to Lorna.

When he places the tray on her lap, she puts her hand on his arm. Her face is fearful, perhaps she knows what's coming after. Joey feels a pang of compassion for her helplessness, but can't do a thing. He just has to hope that social come on the 6th of August, like the letter said, and do something about it. Lorna is not his problem.

Billy pushes his empty plate to the middle of the table. Even that gesture feels loaded. Everything he does is a reminder to others that he is in charge. He pushes back the chair, pats his stomach and says, 'Time for afters.'

He winks at Candace.

Joey is finding Billy increasingly perverse, but makes sure nothing in his expression flickers.

He distracts Candace with the offer of an ice lolly from the freezer, while trying to ignore what he can hear from Billy by the armchair.

'Come on, get up. I need my pudding.'

Joey waits until Lorna has moved to take Candace into the sitting room. He turns the TV up louder than normal, so Candace can't hear her mum being fucked up the backside or whatever other brutalities Billy is in the mood for.

He doesn't want to know.

It doesn't take long. Billy comes from the bedroom, still fiddling with his trousers. He walks past Joey and Candace and looks out of the kitchen window.

'Look, the police have gone home for dinner. Pricks!'

He flips up his hood and leaves the flat, shutting the door behind him with a loud slam. Soon after, the revving of his BMW can be heard in the flat. Joey shakes his head. The man is unreal. Brazen and above the law because he has friends in high places. And, occasionally, in his bed too.

XXI

Joey

By the 5th of August, the day before the scheduled social visit, Joey is doing his best to hide his anticipation, though the thoughts of possible outcomes are consuming him.

He desperately wants Lorna to get the help she needs and for Candace to go into foster care. It will be such a relief not to feel responsible for her anymore. He wants this little girl to be safe and to have a life, a future, some prospects. She won't get it while her mum is permanently off her head and being raped by Billy. Candace needs to go to school and get an education. A real one. Not this street learning. The few letters he's taught her and the stories he's read aren't enough. She needs to play, to socialise, to meet other kids her age, to start to understand what some kind of 'normal' might be. He can't have her, all this, on his conscience any more. It's too much.

And tomorrow could be it. It has to be. Tomorrow is the day.

On the surface Joey seems to carry on as normal. He ploughs on through the work. A delivery out of town to

Woking, Basingstoke and Reading. They're out in the car today, which makes a change from public transport. Candace is by his side in the passenger seat with her rucksack. Shouldn't a kid her age have some sort of car seat? He isn't sure, but he's put a couple of cushions on the front seat so she can see out of the window.

They get through the drops smoothly and leave early. On days like this, when it all goes well, selling drugs is easy, money for old rope. Joey is pleased with their pace and buys them a drive-thru McDonald's for lunch. Candace is content, smiling away, despite spilling sauce down her top. Joey pulls in at the nearby services to buy some wet wipes. He wipes her top down to get rid of the ketchup.

'We don't want wasps in the car, do we?'

'Nope,' she shakes her head, firmly. 'They sting.'

He unzips her front pocket to put in the wet wipes when he notices something attached. He feels it from the outside and knows exactly what it is. It wasn't in there last week because he put her sweets in there and would have seen it. It's an Apple AirTag, a GPS tracking device. Billy — or someone — is tracking him. Watching where he goes. He's got £800 pounds he wants to put in the pink rucksack at the storage facility. Fuck. He thinks for a moment. Then smiles as the answer comes to him. He parks his car in a side street near the station in Clapham, then checks every inch of Candace for another AirTag or GPS device. Sure enough, checking inside Candace's trainers he finds another one. Bastard. He takes out the battery and leaves it in the car. That should disable it. Worst ways it will look as if he's left her there, waiting for him.

They walk to Clapham station and catch the next train to Waterloo. From there they head by foot to Tate Modern. They haven't been for a little while. He'll leave the rucksack in a locker at the Tate, then walk along to Stashy's and put the money in the duplicate bag. His little fund has grown nicely. He's kept his cut small, never ripping the arse out of it. He remembers the hare and the tortoise, his mum's motto that slow and steady wins the race.

She's right. Joey doesn't need to do the calculation to know that he now has over 6k saved. Candace will be taken care of and he'll be free soon to get away. He and Candace only spend a short time at the Tate. He doesn't want the tracker out of action too long. They have their little routine. She has her favourite pictures now, that she likes to return to again and again. But they also choose something new to focus on each time. She likes people, colour, shapes, animals: paintings she can make up stories about. She's less keen on the landscapes. She thinks they're boring and nothing is happening. Perhaps she's got a point. He's not a particular fan of Turner, either.

After they've been round, they make their obligatory visit to the shop where they buy another fridge magnet – she has quite the collection now – and a yellow purse on a neck-string that she was very taken with. It has googly eyes on it, and she likes yellow. He could have chosen it for her, he knows her tastes so well now.

They make their way back to the car where he puts the AirTag back in Candace's trainer with the battery. They have a delivery in Clapham, not far from the car park and, lo and behold, he sees the blue BMW parked on the other side of the road. Whoever these clowns are, they're not very good. He holds Candace's sleeve and walks with her to the corner of the road where there's a crowd of people sitting outside a busy pub. He sees his client and heads over. Deal done, they get back in the car and drive home. He watches for the blue BMW. It appears in his mirror intermittently.

When they get to the flat, the green van that seems to have been in regular attendance, has gone for the day again. These guys only seem to work from 9-5. It wasn't there when he and Candace left this morning, either. If it's surveillance, the effort is minimal.

The cooks are keen to get out of the door and away, as miserable and mysterious as ever. This time, Joey catches a glimpse of their day rate. A thick enough roll of crisp fifties to make 5k. They are making *a lot* of money. You'd think they'd be a bit happier in their work. But, Joey reminds himself, it's nowhere near as much as Billy is raking in.

Candace is wearing her yellow purse with pride. 'Look what I got!'

Billy shakes his head. 'She can't wear that tomorrow. It stays here.'

Joey really hates the way Billy talks about her in the

third person, as though she's not even in the room, and certainly not worthy of his attention. It really gets to Joey.

Candace looks crushed, and Joey feels bad for her, but Billy's tone is final. Candace is smart enough to understand that there's no arguing with Billy. And actually, he's probably got a point. They don't want any distinguishing features. Nothing that would make her stand out from the crowd. Loads of little girls have pink rucksacks, but a yellow purse with googly eyes would be easily remembered. Candace opens the zip of the bag, pulls out her Tate Modern paper bag and puts the magnet proudly on the fridge. It's Roy Lichtenstein's *Mustard on White*. Candace likes it because of the bright colours and, regardless of its title, she has decided that it's someone putting butter on toast – just like Joey does for her most mornings.

'At that fuckin' gallery again?'

Joey shrugs. 'Not long. Flying visit in between drops. Keeps her quiet.'

'And that counts as art, does it? Tell you what, I could fuckin' draw that.'

Candace frowns, but knows better than to speak with Billy in this sort of mood.

Joey hates Billy's unnecessary swearing. Joey swears as much as the next person, but there's no need to make it every other word when you're talking in front of a five-year-old. It wouldn't hurt Billy to tone it down a bit. But he'd never dare tell him that.

'Yeah, well, you get all sorts in that Tate Modern,' Joey says, dismissively.

Billy eyes him up, thoughtfully. Joey hands over today's cash and watches as Billy counts it. Twice. Billy pulls out a £50 note and gives it to Joey. 'Petrol.'

Joey nods.

When the cooks have left, Joey asks who wants dinner.

Billy looks at him and shakes his head. 'No cooking dinner tonight, darling. I've got friends coming over.'

'Who?' The question is on the air before Joey can help himself. That came out a bit quick. He corrects his tone. 'Cos, I mean, have I got time to heat something up quick for the girl?'

Billy glances over at Candace, who's sitting on the sofa, admiring her yellow purse. He pulls out one of the rolls and pulls off another £20 note. 'Tell you what, you two kids go out and get yourselves some fish 'n' chips.'

He passes the money to Joey.

'Take your time. Knock yourselves out. Now scarper, I'm expecting visitors.' Joey hangs Candace's rucksack on the back of one of the kitchen chairs. He's had enough of that bag today.

He moves over to Candace. 'Come on, Candy, let's go and get some dinner.'

'Go to the park, yeah. Don't hurry back. I need a good couple of hours,' Billy says.

His tone is light, but this is all very mysterious and out of character for Billy. Joey is suspicious, he doesn't quite know what to make of it. As always, he feels that being on his guard is the best option.

'Righto.'

As they head down the steps, Joey asks Candace if she wants to go to the park or the chip shop first.

'Park.'

Joey would have preferred it the other way around, his stomach is rumbling. 'Tell you what, if we get the chips first, we can go and eat 'em in the park. As a treat, I'll buy you an ice-cream from the shop on our way home.'

She is easily persuaded. They get their dinner and head through the park gates, sitting on the first bench they come to in order to bolt their food. They are *always* hungry. Every day they walk miles and burn up a load of calories.

Joey puts the paper in the bin and they have a few minutes on the swings, but there is a group of teenagers smoking and laughing in one corner and it doesn't have the same feel in the evening as it does on a sunny afternoon. Candace soon tires of it.

'You said ice cream.'

They walk back toward the shops. The shop that's open at this time of night is the international market. It's so big that it takes up the space of three regular shops in the little parade, set slightly back from the road.

As they walk toward the door of the shop, a motorbike with a pillion passenger rides right up to Joey. The passenger reaches for his pocket. Joey sees what's happening and all his protective instincts kick in. He throws himself over Candace, knocking them both to the floor.

He feels the sting just a fraction before he hears the sound of the bullet.

XXII

Joey

Thank fuck. The bullet has only winged his arm. He almost laughs with relief. His quick movement and their unsteady aim on the bike worked in his favour.

Candace is safe.

But even though they've been shot at, no one helps. No one even reacts. No one says anything. They don't want to get involved. It's that kind of neighbourhood. It's too dangerous. Every shop is paying over the odds for protection and that money will most likely be going to Billy.

Joey stands up and looks around. He checks Candace over. She is crying, shocked, but physically unharmed.

He looks at his arm. It's bleeding a lot, it's a scratch, but it's a warning. A big warning.

He composes himself, takes a deep breath and says, 'Now, how about that ice-cream?'

Candace nods through her sniffles.

They go into the shop. Joey picks up an ice cream and some sweets for Candace, plus a quarter size bottle of Jim Beam and a box of paracetamol for himself, pulling his sleeve tight to stem the blood dripping down his arm. His hands are shaking as he hands over the money. They go back to the park, teenagers or not. They sit on their bench. He knows the gunman will be far from the scene now. Candace leans into him and holds his arm. Joey is more determined than ever to get out of this. He literally can't take this anymore or he'll end up dead. There's no way of knowing for sure if that little performance was arranged by Billy, but Joey knows where he'd lay his money. After all, it was Billy who suggested they went out to the chip shop and he gave him some money to do it – something he never does. But Joey has no choice. He has to go back to the flat.

He swallows a couple of paracetamol, washing them down with the Jimmy, then tries to work out how to play it when they return. He decides to play it down. An inevitable hazard in their line of work. He waits across the road with Candace, curious to see who the visitors are. But he can't see any sign of visitors. That sort of confirms this as Billy's work.

Candace is yawning, barely able to keep herself awake now that the shock has subsided and her stomach's full. They walk past the lift just as it opens and three men get out, heading in the other direction. They don't see Joey or Candace, who quickly dart behind a wall. Joey watches them carefully. They walk out of the car park, their heads down, feet shuffling, as if they're really concentrating. They look different to most people around here. Hippyish, something new age, tree hugging. Not survivors in this urban jungle. They walk up to an old, red VW Golf. The one who climbs into the driver's seat has mad, thick, spikey black dreadlocks, a bit Bob Marley but more jagged. The other two have grown-out, greasy hair and their clothes are dirty and shabby. They all look olive-skinned, Mediterranean but sallow, almost ill-looking, with huge black circles around their eyes. Joey wonders what they could possibly be about. They must have come from the flat, they stink of weed.

When Candace and Joey get to the front door, he breathes deeply, in and then out, bracing himself. Candace copies him. It makes him smile to see her earnestness, in spite of the terror of the evening.

'You're back, then. Did you enjoy your fish 'n' chips?' Billy is smiling. Is there anything more behind it? Joey can't read the smile.

Candace nods and heads towards the sofa.

'We were nearly taken out by some psycho motorbike,' says Joey.

Billy looks up sharply. 'Where?'

Joey describes the spot and the angles.

Billy looks annoyed, but not concerned. 'I'll find out who did that,' he says. As though he's talking about a plant-pot being knocked over, rather than an attempted assassination.

Joey detects the lingering smell of weed in the air. 'Were your guests the three we just met coming up?'

Billy smiles again. 'Yeah, they're our new line, the Portuguese.'

Joey says, 'They're stoners, though.'

'Yep, organic weed. Grown in the West Country. Huge fuckin' business with the healthy middle-aged, who want to use it for aches and pains. Massive up-turn since Covid. All the silver-heads are getting stoned.' He chuckles. 'They are fucking brilliant gardeners, those three, and they know what they're doing.'

Joey realises that Billy is stoned. He's finding everything amusing, and has discovered his hippy side. He starts giggling and chatting about existential crap. Joey's never seen him like this before. He decides he prefers this version of Billy and hopes that it might give Lorna a night off.

Joey should be heading off, but he doesn't feel right about leaving Candace yet. What happened earlier scared the shit out of him, so it must have frightened her.

'Do you want to go and get into your pyjamas and we can watch some Disney?' he suggests to Candace. By the time she returns from the bedroom and the bathroom, Joey has set it up for her. She sits next to him, puts her thumb in her mouth and snuggles up against him on the sofa. He can hear her little heart beating against his chest. She is so alive and vital.

Billy is away with the fairies. He hardly notices that they are there.

A little while later, there's some crashing about in the kitchen, the sound of cupboard doors opening and shutting, drawers being pulled and closed. Candace is totally involved in *Sleeping Beauty*. Joey sits there, wondering what Billy is up to. Perhaps he's looking for the letter that tells him that tomorrow the social are coming. This next bit is in the lap of the Gods.

But Billy walks into the lounge, puts his hands on his hips and asks, 'Have we got any chocolate?'

'No, mate, you do the shopping.' Joey says, keeping his eyes on the screen.

Billy pulls out a roll from his pocket. 'I'll give you £50 if you go and get me a KitKat, Flake, Fanta, and a big bag of orange Doritos.'

For fuck's sake. Billy has turned into some sort of stoned kid. He goes back into the kitchen and calls out, 'And a Lion bar. I fancy a Lion bar. While you're at it, get me a tin of Stella. Naah, get me a bottle of red wine, a nice one. Yeah, cheese and onion crisps, too.'

Joey wriggles away from Candace, who is now lying prone on the sofa, still sucking her thumb, eyes heavy, but still focused on the film. He goes into the kitchen to make a list.

'I'll write it down, Billy, or I'll forget.'

Billy searches the side for a scrap of paper and a pen. He lands on the pile of mail, mumbling about the waste of paper.

'Fucking advertising bollocks.'

He alights on the grey, recycled envelope. 'This'll do.'

He turns it over and finds a pen.

Joey freezes. This is tense. Joey walks over, takes the pen and reaches for the envelope. 'Right, Billy. What d'you fancy?'

Billy runs through his long list of confectionery and wine, adding even more cravings than before. Joey stands up and folds the envelope over to put in his jeans pocket. 'See you in a bit then, yeah.'

Joey walks to the front door and is hit once again by the warm evening air when he opens it. As he goes to pull the door to, he hears, 'Joey, wait. Come ere.'

Joey walks back in.

'That envelope, give it 'ere a sec.'

Something must have registered through the drug-fug. Heart beating hard, Joey hands over the envelope.

'Yeah, thought so. That's from social, that paper. They use that shit.'

Joey feels a partial sense of relief, for his own skin. This is nothing to do with him now, but this is all to do with Candace and Lorna. Joey stands opposite Billy while he reads the letter.

'What's the date today?'

Joey checks his phone, as though the date hasn't been seared into his brain for days.

'5th.'

'Fucking stupid cunt! We gotta sort this flat out and get Lorna sober. She's needs to be fuckin' on this.'

Joey pulls out his best confused face from Year 7 and 8 drama lessons. 'What? What's going on?'

Billy hands him the letter.

'Shit, man, that's tomorrow, 9am.'

Billy is already on it, messaging the cooks not to come in in the morning.

Joey knows that he needs to be on the right side of Billy. As he gets closer to escape, he mustn't put a foot wrong. He says, 'D'ya still want me to get the list?'

Billy is walking around in circles, rubbing the back of his head with his flat hand. Joey knows this is what he does when he's stressed and needs to think.

'Yeah, fuck it. I need some fuckin' sugar.'

'Righto. I'll be right back, mate, and then we can get this flat straight. Yeah, it won't take long.'

He looks over at Candace. She is falling asleep now. He can move her into her bed when he gets back.

Joey shoots down the stairs, through the car park, onto the road and to the mini market. He buys everything on the list, throwing in some extra bits for good measure. He runs straight back, And as he opens the door, he hears the dulcet tones of Billy, shouting at Lorna.

'You fucking useless bitch, you had this letter, you didn't read it!'

He is shaking her by the shoulders. She pukes onto him and then some more onto the bed.

Joey thinks, 'Well, that's just great, another thing I'll have to clear up,' then realises his moral compass is shifting again and the empathy that had started to return has temporarily evaporated. But he also knows it has to, if he's to survive this.

Joey returns holding up the thin blue and white mini-market bag.

Billy's eyes light up.

Joey encourages him into the kitchen and pulls out a chair for him. He sits down. Joey takes all the items out of the bag, and gets him a glass for his wine. Billy seems content and begins to tuck into his banquet, allaying the extreme munchies.

Seeing Billy distracted by his sugar and wine fix, at least for a moment, Joey goes in to check on Lorna. He has always kept a distance from Lorna, physically and emotionally, because, if he's honest with himself, he despises her for being so weak and not paying attention. He thinks she's an arsehole for the position she's put her daughter in. Yet there's a part of him that feels incredibly sorry for her. She's helpless, used by Billy – as they all are. The knowledge that Billy has been raping her repulses him more and more.

He sits on the bed and keeps his voice gentle. A contrast with the shouting and bullying she's usually on the receiving end of.

'Lorna, I'm going to tidy your room. I'll use the hoover, so try and ignore the noise. Don't worry, you don't need to do anything more than sleep this off, but please, in the morning, have a shower and wash your hair. The social workers are coming early, at 9am, to see you and Candy. If we don't put on a good show they will take Candy away. Do you understand that?'

Despite that outcome being exactly the one that Joey wants to see happen, he also wonders if a last-ditch dose of reality might motivate Lorna to look after Candace and get away from Billy. But then he reminds himself, not just of the improbability of that happening, but the impossibility of it. Die or leave the country. Those are the only choices.

He picks Lorna's clothes up off the floor and takes them to the washing machine. Billy is scrolling through his phone, checking all the deliveries happening this evening. Joey feels like he has become one of Billy's little wifeys. There just to do his bidding. At least he isn't being shagged, thank God.

Next, Joey opens all the windows to let out the still-lingering odour of weed. He finishes Lorna's room and lays out some clothes for the morning. He tries to choose an outfit that says a bit more 'mum' and a bit less 'junkie'.

He does a quick tidy-up of Candace's room. Her little yellow purse is under her pillow and he finds himself strangely moved when he notices it. He leaves it there, picks her clothes up and puts them outside the bedroom door. He then drags the hoover in and begins going over the fluffy pink rug. As he vacuums the edge by her bed, he hears the tell-tale clang of something going up the hoover pipe. He turns off the stinking hot hoover and shakes out a small brown bottle of liquid from the hose. On the outside, something's been hand-written on the label. He reads the letters F-E-N-T. Joey picks it up and puts it in his pocket. How the fuck did that end up under her bed? Fentanyl? That would kill her. Somewhere in the recesses of his brain he's read that there are something like 300 deaths a day from Fentanyl overdoses. As little as two milligrams would kill an adult. This little amber glass bottle contains 5ml.

This bottle could kill all of them, let alone a kid. What the actual fuck is it doing in Candace's bedroom? How the hell did it get there? Why didn't anyone notice? How did the cooks not miss a bottle? He's watched them. They're precise as hell. All their little checks and balances and measurements. They're not careless. It doesn't make any sense.

Lately fentanyl has lost some of its street value. The market's always changing and evolving, as Billy's little development with the Portuguese stoner gardeners tonight showed. But fentanyl has become hard to sell, because of the horror stories surrounding it. People are scared of it. The cooks make new recipes that include tinier amounts of it. Kids are buying fentanyl now for as little at £1. Even so, one pill can kill.

Joey takes the bottle to show Billy. His boss has almost finished the bottle of wine and is three-quarters of the way through a sharing bag of Doritos. Joey holds up the bottle.

Billy shrugs.

'Mate, it was under Candy's bed. The cooks must have noticed there was one missing, surely. You run a tight ship, we all know that.'

Billy is now getting drunk as well as stoned, despite having the constitution of an ox – a useful attribute if you are a major drug-dealer. Joey has never seen him like this before.

He holds up his glass as if to make a toast. 'Write *drink me* on it and leave it by her bed.'

Joey's expression must give him away. Billy is nonplussed.

'What? What are you looking at me like that for? She's a fuckin' liability. We lose a whole day tomorrow because fuckin' social are coming to check up on the little runt.'

Joey nearly says, 'That's not her fault!' but reminds himself who he's talking to and that he's playing the long game.

'It'd be easier for everyone if she curled up into a corner and died,' Billy says.

Joey's fingers are itching to hurt the man. How dare he? But he dials right back. 'Yeah, well, I'll give it to the cooks when they're back in.'

Billy grunts.

'Do you want me to take Candy out tomorrow?'

Billy looks up. 'Yeah. The cooks will be here at 11am. They'll need an hour to put a run together. Be ready for 12 o'clock. You can go midtown then. City boys and their crooked lawyers.'

Joey tries to tell himself that not all city workers and lawyers are bent. He's been consciously trying to recondition his thinking, increasingly self-aware about the way that he's been sucked into this darkness. As well as the drawing that is grounding him and returning him to a pre-criminal mindset, Joey has been listening to a podcast called 'I Want To Give Myself A Chance', about rehabilitation and all the agencies that apparently circle around criminals but are there to help.

Joey knows, absolutely, without doubt, that he has to leave the country. Just a few more weeks and he'll have the 10k that he's mentally committed to. A good amount of money to get away. Ireland. Then Europe. Perhaps, one day, Belgium. Where his mum is. He's still got her address somewhere.

In a few months' time, when he's shaken off the filth of this underworld, he's going to start to rebuild some bridges.

XXIII

Candace

Billy gives her mum some white powder for breakfast. It must be good medicine, because she is soon up and showered and smiling. Candace is very pleased to see that her mum is up and about. She has been sleepy for such a long time. Perhaps her mum will play with her today. She used to, on the smiling days.

It would be fun if she joined in her game. They could have a tea party with pretend ice-cream, or do some drawing. Or even bake some cookies together. Candace's favourite days in her life have been those handful of days she can remember when her mum has done those things with her.

'Mu-um, Mummy, play with me,' Candace calls. 'Pleeeeeese?'

It doesn't work. Her mum pays no attention to her request and instead shoos her away with a flap of her hands. 'I haven't got time, baby. Billy's said that we can't fuck this up.'

Candace hates it when her mum uses the bad words, like

Billy does. Joey doesn't do that, even though he sometimes says them when he speaks to other people.

'I need a cigarette. Or a spliff.'

Candace can see that her mum's hands are shaking.

'But I mustn't, 'cos the social workers are coming and I can't fuck-up,' she repeats. Her mum feverishly wipes down surfaces that are already clean.

'Candy baby, when the nice ladies ask you questions about where you go, what will you say?' Lorna asks.

Candace thinks. 'Museums. And art galleries. I go to Tate Modern to look at art and buy fridge magnets so I can remember my favourite pictures.'

'Do you?' her mum sounds surprised. 'That's a good answer. Yes, say that.'

Her mum refolds a tea towel that was already folded.

'Baby girl, you sit over there now and play with your toys.'

'Yes, Mama.'

Lorna rushes up to her suddenly and tucks one of her curls back into her hair. Candace wasn't expecting it and takes a step backwards. Her mum doesn't usually care about her hair.

The knock at the door comes.

The clock in the kitchen says nine o'clock. Joey taught her the hour hand, so she can do the o'clocks.

'Shit. That's them.'

Lorna puts her head in her hands for a moment and then lifts her head up and goes to the door.

'Hello, come on in.' Lorna's voice sounds funny. Too high and squeaky. A man and a woman come into the flat.

'Oh, you're different,' her mum says. 'I thought you would be the other social workers, the ones from last time.'

The man, who introduces himself as 'Danny' smiles and says, 'I'm afraid they're both on leave at the moment.'

'Right. Well, er, would you like a cup of tea?' Lorna asks.

Her mum's voice sounds funny. Like she isn't feeling very well.

Danny wanders over to Candace and kneels down beside her, like the other lady did, and talks about her tea party game.

Danny is older than Joey, but his clothes are brighter. She likes his orange shirt with different sized squares on it. He has a beard, like Billy, but Danny's is grey and trimmed into a neat triangle. He has a bald head, but there are some little bits of red hair around the sides.

'I like your shirt,' Candace tells him. 'It looks like a painting.'

The lady is called 'Nikki' and acts like she is in charge. Nikki goes into the kitchen.

'Oh, you do a good job of keeping this tidy,' Nikki says.

Candace waits for her mum to tell them that it isn't her, it's the cooks who keep it clean and put everything away.

'Is it tea or coffee?' Lorna asks, getting mugs out while the kettle boils.

'Oh, I'm not sure what Danny will have, but a cup of coffee, white, no sugar, for me.'

Lorna drops a cup and Candace winces at the noise as it smashes. Her mum must be nervous, or those shakes have got really bad.

'Whoops. I'm all fingers and thumbs this morning.'

She picks up the pieces and then comes over to Candace and Danny to ask about his drink.

Danny stops playing with Candace for a moment and starts talking about the lovely ornaments. Candace hears the fridge door open and shut. Nikki must be a nosy person, looking in their fridge, or perhaps she's being helpful and getting the milk out for her mum. She knows they have some, because Joey put it there this morning.

Danny also wants coffee, white with no sugar.

Candace's tummy is rumbling. She hasn't had any breakfast yet, but she knows better than to mention that in front of Nikki and Danny.

Lorna goes back into the kitchen, wiping both hands down her legs at the same time. She looks nervous and very shaky. When the coffees are made, she sits at the kitchen table.

Danny keeps asking Candace lots of questions. It's nice to have someone new to talk to, so Candace enjoys giving him long, detailed answers. She tells him about all the art she likes.

'Would you like to see my fridge magnets? I'm starting a collection. I got one from the Sea Life Centre and I got another one from Tate Modern. That's one of my favourite places to go. We go there a lot.'

Her mum sneezes loudly. 'Must be hayfever,' she says. 'We left the small windows open all night and there are those tall fern trees either side of the flats.'

'You don't look well,' Nikki says. 'Are you feeling alright.'

'I'm fine. Just an allergy to the trees. I always get it, it's the trees.'

Her mum does not look fine. She looks hot, and large red lumps are coming up on her neck.

Danny walks towards the sink with his empty coffee cup and puts it on the draining board.

After a bit, Nikki says, 'Well I think that's it. We'll write up a report and send a copy to you.'

When the front door is closed behind them, Lorna tells Candace that she feels dreadful. Her heart is racing. 'I had no idea it would be that stressful.'

Candace watches her mum stagger into the kitchen, where she kind of collapses back into the chair.

'Candy?'

Candace jumps up and goes to the kitchen.

'Baby girl, get mummy some water, could you?'

Candace takes the mug next to the sink and fills it with water. She passes it to her mum, noticing that the water is slightly brown still. Maybe she should have cleaned the cup.

Billy appears. Maybe he was waiting outside for Nikki and Danny to go.

'What happened?' he asks.

'It was good. It was fine.'

Lorna keeps saying the word 'fine', but Candace doesn't believe her.

Billy starts shaking her round the shoulders, like he does sometimes. 'You're a fucking joke,' he says. Then he slaps her around the face. 'What have you done? What have you said to them?'

Lorna tries to shake her head.

Billy slaps her again. 'Wake up, you stupid bitch.'

Candace runs out of the kitchen and throws herself behind the arm of the sofa. She can't look. But she must. Billy seems to be going mad, whacking her across the face and head. Candace pops her head up and sees blood on her mum's face.

She is trying to get away from him, crouching on the chair to make herself small, with her hands on top of her head in a pitiful attempt to try to stop the punches. Billy does not stop. Punch after punch, whack after whack. Candace puts her hands over her eyes to try to stop herself from looking. Billy is like a monster in one of her storybooks. The scary giant who will never stop.

'You're fuckin' useless, a waste of fuckin' space!' he keeps shouting, over and over.

Candace wants to scream but she doesn't want Billy to see her and hurt her like he's hurting her mum. So she puts her fist in her mouth and crawls further behind the sofa. She puts her head against the cold tiles on the ground, and puts a fallen sofa cushion over the top to block out the horrible noises.

She can only cry silent tears.

XXIV

Joey

Just before 11am, Joey appears at the door as arranged, ready to deal with the cooks.

But the first thing he sees is Candace's legs, poking out from behind the end of the sofa.

Something is very wrong.

He puts his index finger up to his lips and holds his left hand out, hand flat, advancing towards her.

She is crying. The poor kid is terrified. Something bad must have happened. Did the social visit not go well?

He winks at her and gives her his warmest smile to let her know that everything is alright.

She just stares back at him, eyes wide, and so wet they look as if they are made of liquid.

He walks backwards, away from her, and then turns as he hears a sound. He sees the back of Billy, leaving the flat through the door. Has Billy seen Joey? Joey thinks not.

When he has gone, Joey lowers himself down and moves carefully towards the kitchen so that he can't be seen through the window. He keeps his left hand stretched out, pumping up and down slowly to indicate to Candace to stay where she is.

He stands by the kitchen door looking in, Lorna is lying across the tiles, blood everywhere. He stands up and runs towards her and is just about to reach down and touch her but decides against it.

His prints are on file. He doesn't want to be involved in this any more than he has to be.

Her nose is twisted, her face is red and purple, and there is blood flowing from her nose and mouth. She is shivering, but alive. Just about.

'Lorna?' There is no response. Her eyes are open but she can't hear him.

He grabs Candace's rucksack, stuffs it with the pyjamas by her pillow, picks up her shoes and calls her towards him.

She moves in his direction and he stands blocking the doorway so that Candace can't see her mum.

'Let's go upstairs, to my place. I'm calling some help for Mummy. We'll wait there.'

He's just about to use his phone, then puts it away. Instead, he pulls out his work phone, a burner that can't be traced, and calls 999.

He walks Candace upstairs, first checking that Billy isn't there. He wouldn't be so stupid after what he's just done.

Joey keeps a lookout, waiting for the ambulance to arrive. He's left the front door open so they can see her. He puts Candace in front of the TV with a big bowl of cereal. She seems okay in herself, though he knows there is no way she can be. The kid must have been completely traumatised by what she's just witnessed. Jesus.

Something must have made Billy snap. Something about the social visit. This is why he has the name Billy Bananas. This uncontrollable, violent temper. He's unstoppable when the red mist descends. Joey saw it once in prison when another inmate upset Billy. The pummelling the other man got nearly killed him. And now Billy has done the same to Lorna. She was in a terrible state. She might be dead now. He doesn't know.

He sees the ambulance arrive outside. Two paramedics run up the stairs and into the flat.

'Mummy's going to be okay, Candace. She's being looked after now,' he tells her.

He has no idea if the first part of that statement is true.

The police are soon behind the paramedics.

Joey has no idea what to do next. What to do with Candace.

Billy will be watching, somehow. If not him, then one of his minions. That is most of the population in the area. They're everywhere. And now they will have eyes on him. He needs to think about what his next move is. They'll know he called the emergency services. What will Billy do next?

Fuck.

He decides to wait and see what happens. He notices the cooks' silver Tesla parking up. They walk in together, up the stairs and along the balcony to the flat – but walk straight past, back down the stairs at the other end. Both are holding their 'materials' briefcases. They walk back to their car and Mr Cook is straight on the phone.

It's obvious Billy isn't answering, from the exasperated faces they make.

They must be furious. They will leave the job now; their skills are in high demand. As freelancers they can go where they want, and this is now a wasted day for them – lost earnings. Billy's operation is going to fall apart without them.

The police will soon realise that Candace is missing, social were there and now Candace is gone.

Joey doesn't know what to do.

He waits to see what happens with Lorna. It's nearly an hour before the paramedics bring her out on a stretcher. The two men have to carry her down the stairs because the lift is broken again. She has her eyes closed and a mask across her face.

Once the paramedics have gone, the police start knocking on the door of the flat next door to Lorna's. They are obviously going door to door to see if anyone has seen anything. You'd be a fool to say you'd seen Billy leaving. But someone might have seen Joey. Either way, it won't take long for them to knock on his door. Joey calculates. They won't want to come in. They can't, not without a warrant.

Joey decides to bite the bullet and call Billy. No answer. Just like that, it seems the whole operation is over.

What to do, what to do? Joey paces around the flat trying to think. Joey knows that Billy keeps a stash of drugs somewhere in the flat, hidden in his old room that he has taken to only using occasionally. Billy has insurance policies everywhere. A stash of drugs is his equivalent of 'rainy day money'.

If he was Billy, where would he have kept a stash? He scans the room looking for likely hideyholes. There's hardly anything in the room. It's like his prison cell. A prison cell with carpet.

The door goes.

Joey can see the police officers through the glass in the door. He pulls the lounge door closed to hide Candace. He hesitates. This is his opportunity to hand her over, for her to go into foster care. But he can't do that right now because he can't be involved. How could he explain her presence in the flat without making himself a suspect? He can't. He needs to stick to his original plan: he is leaving the country. Billy's attack on Lorna just means that Joey needs to bring things forward a little bit. He can drop Candace off somewhere – like a station – in a day or two, and claim that she's lost or something. Then walk away. That will be far safer. He doesn't need to be connected in any way to what went on in that flat.

He opens the front door and looks at the police officer. 'Hello? Can I help you?'

'Good afternoon, Sir. We were just wondering if you know the lady and child from the flat below yours?'

He smiles and says, 'Yeah, Lorna and her little girl. Constance? Something like that.'

He leans against the doorframe, casually, as if he's chatting to a friend at the door, although he feels anything but relaxed. 'Why? What's up? Are they alright?'

The police officer shakes his head. 'No. I'm afraid not. Ms Murphy has been seriously injured. We believe she has been attacked.'

'In her flat? That's awful!'

'It would also appear that the flat was being used to manufacture drugs.'

Joey blows out his cheeks. 'No way.' He pulls a face of shock.

The police officer continues, 'How well do you know Ms Murphy and her daughter?'

Joey says, 'Well, you know, we'd say hello on the stairs if I bumped into her, that sort of thing, you know. I can't say I really know her much more than that. She seemed alright.'

The police officer asks, 'And her daughter, Candace?'

Joey shakes his head. 'Not really. I'd sometimes see her going to the shops with her mum, or going to school in the morning and coming home in the afternoon.'

He mentally kicks himself. That was a stupid answer. Why did he say that? It invites the next question, which tests him.

'That's interesting. What school did she attend, Sir, do you know?'

'No, I don't, I'm afraid I've got no idea, sorry.'

Candace: The Gallery Girl

The police officer isn't finished. 'What colour was her uniform?'

Fuck. Joey is momentarily brought up short, but then it comes to him. 'She wasn't in uniform. Do they wear uniform to little school?'

The police officer seems satisfied that Joey is an out of touch, childless idiot who doesn't know what he's talking about. Joey has played his part perfectly.

He goes back indoors and checks on Candace who holds her empty bowl up at Joey.

'More, please, JoJo,' she says, without looking at him. So much trust. She's so endearing. And so vulnerable.

He resolves to stick to his plan, bide his time and get clear, and make sure she is in care before he leaves. She can't come with him. The last thing he needs is Candace slowing him down. It wouldn't be right anyway. He is a clueless, childless, idiot. He needs to do the right thing by her. He just needs to get her safe.

It's several hours before the work phone rings. Early evening.

'Have you got the girl?' It's Billy.

'Yeah, mate, I have. Thought I'd take her out tomorrow. That's if you got any deliveries. What about the cooks?'

'They've fucked off back to suburbia, the wankers!'

'What's the story with Lorna,' Joey asks. 'The police have been knocking on doors asking questions.'

'Yeah, I know. Don't worry about that. You got the kid. That's all that matters. I've got a buyer.'

Joey isn't sure he's heard Billy right. 'Buyer?'

'Yeah, for the girl. Some weirdo wants her for his wife, you know what I mean.'

Joey feels utterly repulsed. He wants to vomit, but swallows it back. He can't say anything that will jeopardise his plan.

'Righto.'

'There's a stash in my room. Look under the carpet in the far-right corner.'

Joey knew he would have had a stash.

'Pull back the tile underneath. It's in the concrete, inside a box.'

Joey says, 'Yeah, right.'

'Get the kid out working tomorrow. All day, I want her tired. Yeah, I'll send you where I want you to drop her. It's in Surrey, a house that holds little girls like her. They get picked up once a week and they drive down the M5 and the A30. A boat takes a load of 'em every week, see, off to Ireland, then to her new home.'

Joey's stomach is turning. This man is a monster. But somehow he keeps his tone light. 'Cool. Do you want me to see if there's a passport in the flat?'

Of course there won't be a passport in the flat. Candace has never been anywhere in her short little life. Lorna wouldn't have been capable of applying for a passport; she couldn't even register the birth of her own kid, or get her into school.

'Naaah, mate. Like the thinking, but there's no need. We get them made. Hers'll be waiting at the house in Surrey.'

Joey swallows again. 'Yeah, man. Righto. All cool, you'll send the location, yeah? I'll take her over.'

Billy says, 'Good attitude, mate. She's worth a lot of money. Keep her fed, but tired, gottit?'

When the call is over, Joey sits down, tapping the phone against the back of his hand.

How the fuck does he get out of this?

XXV

Joey

Joey digs out the drugs from Billy's hiding place and goes through the packages. He calculates that there might be 5k of coke and MDMA, drugs for the working professionals. More coke than MDMA. Billy must have been planning a night out with some rich friends. Who's he kidding? Joey knows that Billy doesn't have friends, only people with transactional purpose. Like his fuck buddy from children's social care. Who knows? And now this idea to sell Candace.

Billy wants money rolling in every day. That's his primary addiction. Every day he wants profits. He wants his slaves to work every day. He wants to be the big man.

The amounts and split of the drugs feel like the Shoreditch drop: young media people who got their degrees and debt and now spend their money on expensive rent and partying, hoping that they'll get a lucky break.

He gets Candace ready for bed. She can sleep in his bed; he'll take the couch. He doesn't expect to get much sleep. He's right. When Joey closes his eyes he has flashes of that morning running through his mind like a film reel. Lorna's blood-covered face in close-up. When he replays it, he zooms in on the detail he must have registered at the time: some of her teeth lying in the pool of blood by her head.

Billy is a beast, a predator. A vicious bastard. He's had plenty of blood on his hands over the years, but usually he's far away from the scene of the crime. This was vicious and personal and the blood on his hands is literal.

Joey knows his former cellmate. Billy will be hyper-vigilant and hyper-protective of himself. He also won't entirely trust Joey. Joey knows far too much.

Joey must not believe a single word Billy says to him.

After all the things that have happened this week, Billy will be on an adrenaline high. The new deals, the booze, and then beating Lorna to within an inch of her life.

Thoughts circle round and round Joey's mind. They all go back to Billy. Billy will always want to make more money, because that's what he does. His addiction is money, more, more, more. People like Billy, with their bad childhoods, didn't learn to break the cycle. All people like him do is become more ambitious, to play the cycle harder, while never recognising that's what they are doing. Billy is imprisoned in the cycle. Billy is a child trapped inside a man's body; a hurt, frightened child who has survived by defending himself – through taking all the power, by making sure he has everything. Billy despises all others, especially people who he sees himself in. The best outcome for Billy right now is for Joey to disappear and Candace to be sold – gone.

He will want Joey dead.

By the small hours of the morning, Joey knows that.

In the morning, Billy sends over a text. *Piccadilly Circus, West End, sending details.*

Joey chews his lip as he works out how to organise the day.

He goes into his bedroom to wake Candace, who does a giant yawn and a big stretch. His heart flips, but today he needs her. Today, the only protection he has is Candace and the cameras. He has got to stay as public as he can. In London, there is face recognition technology and surveillance nearly everywhere. Nearly a million cameras across the capital. The average person is supposed to be caught on camera something like 70 times a day. For the last few months, CCTV has been the thing to avoid.

Today it will be his friend.

Joey is not under suspicion with the authorities. Billy is the one the police will be after. Billy must have left his DNA in that flat, way more than Joey. Billy's fingerprints will be on the glass he used for his wine, on the doors, on the crisps and chocolate wrappers. His fingerprints and DNA will be on and in Lorna. Billy is in a desperate situation. He can't be seen or he'll be arrested. But desperate men do desperate things.

Joey has to be very, very careful.

He loads up Candace's pink rucksack and leaves it in the kitchen. She needs fresh clothes. He has the spare key to the flat that Billy keeps here, but there'll be police everywhere, forensics crawling over the place.

He goes down to check it out. He can always play the role of the concerned neighbour if anyone questions him. He's surprised to discover that there are no police at all. Joey was expecting loads of press, police, drama. But there is nothing: not even a young beat police officer standing outside hoping their parents bring them a packed lunch.

Lorna is clearly *not* a priority. Another messed up junkie. Unless forensics have been and gone. If that's the case, they will have worked out, or soon will, that drugs were being manufactured in the kitchen – despite the fastidious work of the two cooks, who will themselves have disappeared without trace.

He bends down so no one can see him. He opens the door just enough to squeeze through. He takes a small pile of clean clothes for Candace. For some reason he can't quite fathom, he also takes the framed hairdressing certificate that Lorna keeps on the wall.

He leaves as surreptitiously as he came, bending back down and creeping towards the other stairs at the far end. He goes up a level to get to his floor and door. Again, he bends down so no one can see him. He goes inside and says to himself, 'It's so easy.' Then checks himself. It's the sort of thing that Billy would say. Once, he wanted to be just like Billy. Not anymore.

There are alerts on his phone. Billy is messaging him.
You good?

Joey replies, *Yeah, all set. Just leaving.*

Joey sorts some clothes out for Candace. She's happy with the selection he has brought. He also has her yellow purse. It's tucked into the bottom of the rucksack. He checks the bag for AirTags. He checks *everything* for AirTags. He assumes that Billy's minions will have put a tracker on his car, too. That's the bit he still needs to think about very carefully.

He walks through the car park with Candace. She reaches up for his hand, but he doesn't hold it.

'In a minute, Candy,' he says, looking straight ahead.

There is hurt in her eyes, but he can see the blue BMW. He knew they'd be watching and, so far, he has not given cause for concern. He doesn't want to seem affectionate towards Candace while anyone is looking. Joey is doing everything Billy wants.

Billy is just buying time for himself by sending them off to work today. Joey hopes there aren't any other nasty surprises in store.

They get the bus, then the tube to Piccadilly. A text comes through telling him to go to the food hall arcade.

They wander up to the arcade where they meet a woman who takes them inside a shop. They release 2k's worth of cocaine. Joey does not take a cut of the deal today. He will give Billy nothing at all untoward to focus on. He doesn't want to put a foot wrong.

Candace: The Gallery Girl

With the major deal done, they walk to the West End. Joey assumes that he is being followed by other minions. The BMW wouldn't have been able to get here in time through London traffic. He is vigilant, looking in all the windows as he walks by, trying to spot likely-looking candidates. Everyone comes under suspicion.

Candace is quiet. She is tired. More than tired. She is broken by what has happened in the last 24 hours. She looks up at Joey. 'Are you sure Mummy will be alright?'

He squeezes her hand. 'Yeah, Candy, she's fine. She's not feeling very well today, but she's being looked after and she's not in any pain and she's, er, gettin' better.'

He hates himself for lying. He has no idea if she will be alright, or even where she is. All he knows is that the police will be looking for Candace – and for Billy. He rockets through the West End as quickly as he can. He needs to get to Blackfriars and change rucksacks at the luggage lock-up before they're missed. They only have a small window of opportunity.

He walks past Liberty, towards Carnaby Street. He gets another text from Billy with the next location details. He's got to go into the big white pub and make his way toward the toilets. It's packed with punters, and no one seems to notice a little girl walking through with him. He does his delivery as instructed and takes £500. The next drop is in a restaurant. He takes Candace by the hand for speed and safety. It would be so easy to lose her in the crowd. For her own sake, perhaps that's what he should do. It has to be better than driving Candace to Surrey later to be sold as a sex slave. But would Billy buy that?

Joey knows what the answer is. If he doesn't do what Billy says, he'll be killed, and so will Candace.

He tries not to think about the logistics of what will happen later. It makes him feel queasy, but what can he do? He doesn't have many options. Perhaps he could call the police about the house in Surrey before he gets there. Or alert them just after he's made the drop? He can't just abandon Candace. He needs to protect her. But how?

By 3pm there are just two more drops left to do in the West End. He's worked out now who their tail is. He can see them: two more minions in black hoodies. They're so conspicuous, it's almost laughable.

Ahead of them is a huge vintage clothes shop, where those two will stand out like a sore thumb. That's exactly what Joey needs. The store staff will be watching them, they'll be seen. Joey holds Candace's hand and walks downstairs to a huge space full of rails of clothes from the 70s, 80s and 90s. He wasn't born during the first two decades, and it's funny to think that people were wearing this shit on the 90s rail at the time he was born. He pretends to look through the rails and holds items up to show Candace, who is excited about looking at dresses, hats and sunglasses.

The two minions stand around looking uncomfortable and out of place. They are seen almost instantly by the security staff, who start to follow them, just as Joey hoped.

Candace: The Gallery Girl

Joey edges toward the stairs, so that he and Candace can go up and out of the door and across to the food arcade where they won't be easily found. For good measure, Joey walks up to the very hip young woman at the counter and says, 'Heads up, I just saw those two put somethin' under their hoodie.'

She thanks Joey and calls her security colleagues on their walkie talkies.

Joey is by the stairs, ready. As the security staff approach the two minions, he takes his opportunity to get out of the shop.

It's so easy.

They go back through the arcade. There are still drugs in Candace's backpack, but Joey wants to aim straight for Blackfriars while the coast is clear. He flags a black cab and they're soon speeding away from the area – 20 minutes later they are at Blackfriars and walk quickly to Stashy's. Candace knows the route and asks no questions.

Joey pulls the duplicate pink rucksack from the locker. He puts it on the floor by his feet, and takes the other rucksack from Candace's back. He removes a small vase from it, the one that Lorna had put out of Candace's reach when they first gave the flat a makeover.

Candace recognises it immediately.

'Hey, that's from home.'

'Yeah, I'm keeping it safe while Mummy's away,' he lies again, as he rolls it up in Candace's spare clothes and puts it in the other, stashed pink rucksack, resting on top of his cash. He pulls out the mustard yellow baseball cap he took from the tourists at the Tate. It seems like a long time ago. He puts the drug rucksack inside the locker and puts the new rucksack on his shoulder, the cap on his head. He takes Candace's hand once more and they head out the door.

They walk along the Southbank towards Waterloo station.

'You're going too fast,' Candace complains.

'We gotta, today, Candy. Trust me.' He winces as he asks her to trust him.

On the corner, near the restaurants, is a trendy gift shop. He darts inside, and, with cash from today's takings stowed in his manbag, he buys a cap for Candace and a little blue jacket. There is a large, plain-looking navy rucksack with a trendy logo on the top shelf. He buys all of it. They go into the Italian café next door and get a seat inside, tucked in the corner.

Carefully, he takes out the little vase and positions it on the table so he can take a photo of it with his phone. He sends it to Colin, the man who sells antiques and does interiors. He has an idea about what it could be worth. He then rolls it back up into Candace's clothes and puts it back on top of the money. He has 3k in his manbag, plus the money he's already stashed. Just shy of his 10k target, but events have forced his hand. He puts the pink rucksack inside the new navy rucksack to hide it.

The waiter comes over to take their order. 'One hot chocolate with marshmallows and a latte, please.'

Candace: The Gallery Girl

Candace rubs her tummy and complains of hunger. It's past lunchtime, but Joey doesn't want to stay too long; he scans the counter and says, 'Piece of cake?' praying she's happy with that, rather than a meal that they really don't have time for. Candace looks at a plate on a tray coming from the kitchen to another customer and points at it.

'That one.'

'Tiramisu ice cream cake? Good choice,' The waiter says.

Joey's phone pings. It's from Colin. That was quick.

Rather splendid piece, old chap. Can you take a picture of the base? I'm looking in particular for any writing. And a shot of the inside, if you can.

Joey delves back into the rucksack and discreetly pulls out the vase once more, to take the pictures as instructed. The base that has some scratchy red symbols on it, which is the closest thing Joey can see to writing. He takes shots of the inside from a couple of angles and puts it straight back in his bag. He sends the pics and prepares to wait. The coffee comes, along with hot chocolate and the ice-cream cake. Joey sips his coffee, then leans back against the wall seat while Candace tucks into hers. She seems to be taking her time today, or perhaps it's just that he's conscious of every second ticking away. When she's finally finished, Joey pays and they leave, heading in the direction of Waterloo.

His phone pings and Joey reaches for it, hoping it's the antiques man.

It's Billy.

Joey's heart sinks.

What the fuck are you up to?

Joey ignores it. The truth is, he's not sure he even knows the answer to that question himself.

Over the road, he sees a phone shop. They cross over and go inside so that he can buy another burner phone. He can add all the numbers he needs when they're on the train.

Candace wants him to play 'I Spy' on the train, but he can't do it properly because he's busy sorting the numbers. They usually play a phonetic version, because she still doesn't know her alphabet, but he just doesn't have time today.

'You're not listening!' Candace accuses. 'Why aren't you playing properly?'

'I'm sorry, Candy. I've got to sort some stuff out. Can you do some drawing instead?'

'We haven't got any pens!'

They change trains at Woking, and Joey puts both the old phones on a South Western Railway train, heading to Portsmouth Harbour.

Billy's tracking him via a phone. He must be. That'll give him something to think about and may buy Joey a little bit more time.

They take another train straight back to Waterloo, then over to King's Cross, where they book themselves into a Premier Inn and wait. Joey doesn't think they've been followed. He hopes he's sent Billy on a wild goose chase to Portsmouth.

He pays cash for a week's stay at the hotel, a triple room. Candace can take the double bed and he'll have the single. He still isn't sure exactly what he's going to do, but at least they have a safe base now, and at least Candace isn't going to be dropped off and sold as a sex slave.

That's it. There's no going back now.

Joey *really* needs to think.

XXVI

Joey

Joey lies on the bed with his arms behind his head. Candace is sitting cross-legged at the end of the bed in front of the TV. She is delighted with the room, thinks the pillows are big and fluffy and wants to know if they are going to live here forever.

'Not forever. People stay in hotels when they're on holiday.'

'Are we on holiday?'

'Yeah, sort of. Yeah, we are, we're on holiday.'

Candace hasn't mentioned Lorna again, a small mercy for which he's thankful.

'What do people eat when they're on holiday?'

Joey suddenly realises he hasn't eaten anything all day and notices how hungry he is. He looks at his phone. It's 6pm and Candace has only had a bowl of cereal first this morning and a piece of ice-cream cake in the café. She must be starving, too.

There's a menu on the side in the room, advertising the food in the restaurant downstairs. There's no room service.

He scans the kids' section of the menu for Candace. It'll do. As long as the restaurant is quiet, it should be safe enough to use. No one knows where they are.

'Time for food. Toilet and hands,' he instructs.

Candace gets up from the bed and goes to the bathroom to do as she's told. Joey flicks through the channels while he waits for her. He alights on the news.

A 24-year-old woman has died today in hospital, following a brutal attack at her home. Police believe she was murdered by a drug gang who were using her home to produce drugs.

A picture of Lorna flashes up on the screen.

Joey can feel his eyes go wide. He turns down the sound so that Candace doesn't hear anything from the bathroom and reads the subtitles. The report gives Lorna's name and then says that police are now looking for Lorna's five-year-old daughter, Candace Murphy, who has not been seen since the attack. They haven't put up a picture of Candace. Thank God.

Joey's heart is racing.

Fuck. He feels very sad for Candace. A little bit sick. Poor kid. Her mother's dead and she witnessed her murder.

But, in some ways, this horrible development could spell good news for him and work in their favour. If this is all over the media, Billy will be gone – into hiding with more to think about right now than a few grand missing and tracking them down. This could be the diversion he needs. Joey is more tired than he can ever remember being, but also fully alert, which is an exhausting combination.

Food will help him plan their next steps. He wears the mustard hat in the restaurant, hoping he won't be remembered for anything other than wearing a mustard-coloured cap. Tomorrow he will find another cap or hat. Maybe have his braids cut off, that's a good idea. Shaved head and a beanie. That will help him disappear.

They take a table tucked away in a corner. Joey is salivating at the smell of meat and chips, which is mostly what the restaurant is offering. He decides that he'll order a pint of larger, a 12oz sirloin with peppercorn sauce, skin-on chips and garlic mushrooms.

Candace looks at her menu and points out some of the letters he taught her, but still can't read properly yet. At least that means she won't be able to read about the death of her mother. He reads out the things he thinks she might like.

'They've got chicken burger, or beef burger, or hand-battered fish.'

'What's hand-battered?'

Joey swallows. The first thought that comes to mind is what Billy has done to Candace's mum. He pushes the thought as far away as he can.

'It just means crispy batter, like we had when we went to the fish and chip shop.'

'When the scary motorcycle came?'

Joey swallows again. What kind of a life this kid has had so far.

'Don't think about that. They also got 10-veg tomato

pasta. That sounds good. Nice and healthy. Why don't you have that? Or there's spaghetti bolognese or chicken breast. Everything comes with skin-on chips.'

'Do I like skin-on chips, JoJo?'

'Yeah, you will.'

'I want the same as you.'

'Course you do.'

'Steak, please,' she says to the waitress.

'And peas,' Joey adds.

Candace makes a face. 'Do I have to have peas?'

'I thought you wanted the same as me.'

The waitress smiles. 'Would you like a drawing book and pencils?'

Candace nods quickly.

'And something to drink?'

Joey steps in and says, 'Diet coke will be fine, thank you.'

The waitress is very friendly and seems to have taken a shine to Candace. 'What's your name?' she asks.

Candace opens her mouth and gets as far as, 'Can—' before Joey jumps in over the top of her to stop her saying her full name. 'Candy.'

'Aww, that's lovely. As sweet as Candy.'

Joey smiles as the waitress goes off to fetch the colouring book and pencils. He goes through his new phone, hoping to find a message from the antiques man. He sends Colin the new phone number and a message comes in quickly.

Hi Joe, my first thought is it's Japanese. It's been painted with enamel and it has the signature crackled glaze of the Satsuma make. I've put some feelers out and have quotes in the 10 – 15k range.

Joey lights up at this news.

He'll have more than enough money to start a new life overseas.

'You shouldn't be looking at your phone at the table,' Candace accuses. 'That's what you tell me.'

'You're right, Candy. It's poor behaviour from me.'

But how quickly can he get the money? And what does he do about Candace? Maybe he can take her to a police station or somewhere and drop her off. First thing in the morning.

A few minutes later, another text comes in from Colin.

There is an auction at one of the big houses in 2 days. My associate has suggested that this piece could go up there. I'm sure we can come to a little arrangement about a fee, though the auction house will want 2.5% plus VAT.

The waitress comes to clear their plates. 'Would you like some dessert?'

Candace nods. 'Yum, yes please.'

'Sweet tooth, eh? Candy for Candy! I'll come back with the menus,' the waitress says, laughing.

Joey wishes she wasn't quite so friendly. He doesn't want them to be remembered. And he has business to sort out.

'I'm going to send one more text message,' Joey promises, when she's gone. 'Just one. I wouldn't do it if it wasn't important.'

'Is it about Mummy?' Candace asks.

That brings him up short. 'No, it's not. No word about Mummy, yet.' He swallows. He doesn't know how much longer he can keep up these lies.

He writes another text to Colin. For all Joey's street-knowledge, he hasn't got a clue how the auction houses work.

What do you think it would go for? What if it doesn't sell?

The three dots appear to show that Mr Colin Antiques is composing his reply.

Worse case it doesn't sell, you still have a Satsuma worth 10k. If it lifts, and the Americans and Russians love this stuff, who knows? The sky is the limit!!!

Joey has 2k of cocaine in the room that he wants to get rid of. Antiques man always has an event or party for his clients that he wants coke for. That could work out very nicely indeed. A fair trade, and a good way to ditch the drugs.

Joey scratches his chin and texts back. *Okay, what do I do next?*

He knows he sounds desperate, but Colin will already have worked out that this is probably stolen and that Joey wants cash fast. Joey just hopes that little soft spot the man seems to have for him will work in his favour.

I've arranged with my associate that you can bring the piece to the auction house on the day of the sale. I'll get back to you with the details.

Joey says he can have 2k of coke 'for his trouble' and Colin seems more than satisfied with that.

Both Candace and Joey enjoy chocolate brownies and

ice cream for pudding. Joey pays their bill and leaves a generous tip, hoping that will keep the waitress quiet. Then he worries that it will make them more memorable if she sees the news about Candace missing. He's overthinking everything.

They head back to their room. Joey decides that it will be safest if they stay holed up here, not leave the hotel until they go to the auction house.

'We'll have a day off tomorrow, okay, Candace? No trips out. 'Cos we're on holiday.'

'Yippee!'

She falls asleep in front of the television. Joey thinks about disguises and what he can do to make them both look different. Joey needs to not be recognised by anyone connected to Billy. Candace needs to avoid being recognised as the missing girl on the news.

He wonders how Candace would feel about wearing different clothes. It would be much easier if he could dress her up to look like a boy.

They go down for breakfast in the morning. Candace is in her element at the buffet; she has never seen so much food! Joey is relieved to see that there's no sign of last night's waitress.

He leaves Candace in the hotel room. She's full up from breakfast and content to sit watching TV. She pats her stomach, happily.

'Look, I'm fat!'

She hasn't mentioned her mum this morning, or asked

about going home. He doesn't know what answers he'll give if she does.

He puts on the mustard yellow baseball cap and hangs the 'Do Not Disturb' sign on the outside door handle of the room. He walks a few streets until he spots a barbershop on a sidestreet. He only hesitates a moment before asking to have his braids cut off. As he watches them drop to the floor, he feels strange. Bizarrely, he feels more like himself. He is given a short all-over cut that looks great. His hair was distinctive. Now he looks very different, almost unrecognisable.

In the King's Cross station area there is a kids' clothes shop. He enters, looking for boy's clothes – summer trousers and t-shirts. He buys a selection, and a patterned bucket hat. It will be a very different look from the unicorn baseball cap. There's also a men's clothing shop nearby. He pops in and buys two summer cotton shirts in a style that he'd never normally wear, plus two pairs of chino-style trousers and a pair of brown leather sandals that are so far removed from the trainers he's always worn that he almost laughs. But, actually, after putting them on, he thinks his feet feel lovely and cool in comparison to the heat and restriction of the trainers he's always lived in. Perhaps he could get used to them. He buys three different coloured caps, a trilby, and a lightweight jacket. He zips over to The *Harry Potter* Shop, because he realises that Candace will need to carry her stuff. They're accumulating quite a lot. He buys her a dark blue rucksack. It's a world away from what she'd choose, but he'll make a game of it. Perhaps she'll be swayed by the

Harry Potter thing. She's such a good kid, she'll play along.

Joey goes back to the hotel, constantly checking to see if anyone is following him. Despite being on the run himself, Billy will still have people out after him. And maybe, if Lorna isn't a priority, if her death is dismissed as unimportant because she's a junkie, maybe the police won't have got results back yet from the fingerprints.

Joey lurks in front of shop windows, checking in all directions to see if any minions are around. When he thinks back now, Joey is pretty confident that the motorbike incident was commissioned by Billy. He likes to make an example of people by wounding them or killing them, just to remind others that he is boss. No doubt word is now going round that Joey is in trouble. If that's what Billy was doing before he had any evidence that Joey had double-crossed him, Joey has a pretty good idea of how much that would escalate now. The pillion shooter would be shooting to kill this time round.

But Joey feels okay, there's nothing to see in the reflections. He doesn't think he's been discovered. Yet. And he barely recognises himself, so good luck to anyone else trying to find him. He heads back up to the room. When he walks in, Candace is lying on her front, her face resting in her hands, her legs gently swaying. She looks calm and relaxed. Happy even. Blissfully unaware of all the shit going on around her.

She turns and leaps up in alarm when she sees Joey.

'What's the matter?'

'I didn't know it was you! JoJo, you look like a man!' she gasps, as she finally recognises him with his new look.

Joey wonders what that means, coming from this five-year-old, perhaps six-year-old. What did she think he looked like before?

He takes it as a compliment.

'Thanks.'

Or maybe it isn't, given the men she's known in her life.

'I've done a bit of shopping and I've got you some new clothes, too,' he says. 'And I think, if you're up for it, I'd like to do your hair differently. Kind of like dressing up.'

She smiles. 'Okay, JoJo.' She sits up as Joey lifts up the *Harry Potter* carrier and shows her the rucksack. She gasps again and opens her hands to take it.

'It's new!' she says.

Most of what she's had in her life has come from charity shops, second-hand, he realises.

She holds it on her lap and examines it.

Meanwhile, Joey opens up the clothes shopping bag and holds up the different items to show her. Candace loves each and every one and is quite happy to go along with Joey's plan to walk her around dressed as a boy, taking it as fun.

She hugs all of the items, putting her face into the fabric and inhaling. 'They smell so *new*,' she repeats. 'Thank you, Joey.'

They sit in the room for the rest of the morning, watching TV, hanging out, playing silly games. He is only paying cash, so there is no trail anywhere of their presence. Billy has fingers in the police pie, too. He has people on his payroll to get information when he needs it. Or to lose information if that suits his purpose better. Will he still get away with that now he's a murderer?

Joey also wonders what happened at the address in Surrey when they didn't turn up. They must know what's going on. He wonders who 'they' are. The eastern Europeans are pretty big on trafficking, but then there are the Irish groups, too, and the Welsh. As Joey thinks about it, he wonders how many people there are left in the UK, or indeed the world, who are not involved in some way.

It's lunch time. He hasn't checked the time, but it must be because Candace is complaining of starvation, in spite of her mega-breakfast. Before they go down, he decides to take a quick shower. Joey goes into the bathroom and catches sight of his hair. He likes it even more, he decides. He doesn't know why he hasn't done it before now. And it's zero maintenance. He puts on his new clothes and, as he looks in the mirror, he sees a glimpse of a future in the man looking back at him.

Tomorrow is the auction and, who knows? He might be 10k richer, which would mean over 20k to start a new life. He still hasn't decided on where to go. He thinks about Spain, but knows that too many gang bosses live out there. He thinks about Greece or Croatia, he's after sunshine. There's been too much rain. Maybe he could teach English as a foreign language. It's going to be difficult going anywhere with his criminal record. He contemplates

Scotland, or Wales, maybe southern Ireland. He read that there are non-extradition countries that he could go to; countries who don't have treaties or agreements with the UK, meaning they may not hand over individuals wanted for crimes in other countries. Places like Brunei, Russia, the Gulf States, Montenegro, Ukraine, Moldova, Vietnam, Ecuador, Ethiopia. Joey tries to imagine himself in some of these countries. With 20k he could live like a king in some places. He still doesn't know what he'll do when he gets there. He thinks he'd like to help people. He really is looking for atonement of some kind. Fuck it, maybe he'll just sit on a beach and draw.

He used to lie on his bed in his prison cell and plan his future, the cell where he first met Billy. Looking back, he knew within a split second that Billy would control him, be his master. Joey has disliked himself ever since for allowing that to happen.

But, if anyone knows about the reality of this world of County Lines, it's Joey. He has gradually come to understand that it's the worst of capitalism and slavery. There will never be 'County Lines Lives Matter', like the Pride support network of the LGBTQI+ movement. County Lines is a demoralising, diminishing, utterly terrifying juggernaut of an organisation that enslaves you, then criminalises you. It shouldn't be allowed to happen. But it does. And people in high places let it happen.

But soon he'll escape. Soon he'll be free.

And, somehow, he has to get Candace to safety.

XXVII

Joey

They spend another night in the hotel. Joey is on edge, waiting, thinking, planning. In the morning, after breakfast, Candace watches TV. She doesn't seem to mind.

'It's nice being on holiday, isn't it?'

Joey laughs, his tension momentarily broken. 'Yes, it is.' She has such a funny way of looking at the world. Hardly surprising, given what she's experienced of it. And, given how hard she's had to work these last few months, pounding the streets of London, this really is a holiday.

He goes backwards and forwards, bringing up nice treats which she loves. She is quite easy to keep happy. That's what kids who've never had much are like.

Joey waits to hear from Antiques Colin. He feels agitated not knowing quite what the plan is. He needs to think about how he is going to get across town, to wherever this auction house is.

He feels like a coiled spring.

He's worried for his life and for Candace's, and perhaps he hasn't done the right thing by bringing in Colin. He's broken his own motto of not trusting anyone. After all, Antiques Colin was hosting a party for people from the Epstein orbit. He keeps knocking these thoughts around in his head. It could all be too dangerous. Jeopardise the escape plan. He almost decides to pull out and keep the vase for later, approach someone else somewhere else, maybe up north. He keeps toying with Scotland. £10k is a nice little start for now. The vase could be insurance.

'Sit down, Joey,' Candace says.

She's right. He needs to calm down. Just bide his time.

Before lunchtime, Joey is surprised to find that he's hungry once more. It's strange how hungry you can get when you do nothing all day and know there's nice food on tap. Not like prison, where the food was definitely part of the punishment.

His phone pings, finally.

It's antiques Colin. *Hi Joey, I hope you are well and enjoying the sunshine. All set for tomorrow, here's the postcode. It's an established auction house, all kosher, just bring yourself and the vase, and of course, Candace if she would like to join us, it's a fascinating place – she may enjoy it.*

Uh oh. Joey can't help but feel like this is a trap. Why else would he mention Candace? Why is he trying to make sure that Candace is there? Is someone set up to take her? Has Billy noticed the missing vase? Has he been in touch with Colin to try to track down his lost 'sale'. What does a little girl like Candace sell for? Joey dreads to think. How low is Billy actually lying? Is he still trying to run parts of his business, even though the flat 2 kitchen is gone and he's almost certainly a chief murder suspect?

Joey suspects he knows what the answer is.

Billy's addictions are money. Money and power.

Joey messages back. Even if it's a trap, especially if it's a trap, he has to keep the ruse going. *What time shall we meet you?*

The reply soon pings in.

Get there just before 1pm. The picture went in yesterday and has already created a bit of interest.

Joey feels very uneasy, more and more convinced it's a trap.

What time is it being auctioned? he texts.

Again, the reply comes straight back. *Your item is lot number 7, so I'm guessing it will be around 1.15pm.*

Joey sends the thumbs up emoji.

In the afternoon, he begins trying out different hairstyles on Candace. 'I like playing hairdressers. Mummy was a hairdresser.'

Joey smiles, but he feels a sharp stab of pain every time she mentions her mum.

He combs her hair into as sleek a ponytail as he can tease it into. It's wild and unruly and reminds him of the braids he's just had cut off. If he had a daughter, she'd probably have hair like this. It takes an hour, sitting on the bed behind Candace, combing and brushing her hair into this creation. Once he gets it as flat as he can, he twists the ponytail into a kind of flat bun, so that she looks like a boy and can still wear a cap, or the bucket hat. Without the pink, she can pass for a boy. People see what they want to see.

She thinks for a minute. 'Do I have a different name when I'm pretending to be a boy?'

'Do you want a different name?'

'I could be Brian like grandpa, or Reg like my dad,' she says, uncertainly.

He almost laughs out loud. He won't keep a straight face if he has to call her 'Brian', but Reggie might work. It could kind of suit her.

When they go down to dinner in the evening, Joey is no longer hungry. The stress and anxiety are eating him up. He quickly checks to see that the waitress from the first night isn't working, she would definitely have something to say about Candace's transformation from girl to boy. Candace burbles away, still excited by having so much choice of delicious food and fizzy drinks.

Tonight may well be his last supper. Even though he has no appetite, he orders the biggest steak they've got. Is this how the inmates on Death Row feel?

XXVIII.

Joey

Although he's awake from dawn, Joey waits until 7am to turn on the news, leaving the volume down so he doesn't wake Candace. There are reports from around the world: conflict, casualty, tragedy, but no mention of a murder in London. He breathes out, finally, and is just about to head to the bathroom for a shower when he sees another picture of Lorna Murphy and its caption: *the murdered young mother who police believe was being controlled by a local drugs gang.* He turns the volume up a fraction to hear the report.

Police are looking for this man, Billy O'Shea.

Billy's mugshot flashes up on screen.

He is in his mid-30s, already known to the police and is believed to be dangerous. The public is asked not to approach this man directly, but to call 999 or 101 or report sightings anonymously to Crimestoppers 0800 555 111.

Joey almost laughs, 'Yeah, right. 'Cos you guys are totally legit.'

There is no mention of Candace this time, which is curious, but useful, given that they need to be out and about in public today to get across London to the auction house.

Billy must be doing his nut, because there is no way he can contact Joey. Those phones went in the bin, or at least, on a train heading towards Portsmouth. Joey smiles, imagining Billy walking around in circles, punching things, or people, because things are not in his control.

And Joey knows exactly how much Billy hates that.

Billy will have got everyone he has out looking for Joey – which is why Antiques Colin could well be working for Billy.

He's so torn. The auction house is a proper venue. He's searched it. Overnight, Joey imagined what the set-up there would look like. He's been in an auction house once, when he was a kid with his mum and auntie. They were buying old furniture for his auntie's new home, a big white house in the countryside. Auntie Eunice had married this white guy, a businessman, who ended up treating her like shit, like she was staff. Joey remembers his uncle had three kids around his age from a past marriage. He'd hang out with them when they were on visits. He remembers his mum helping his auntie leave the house one day, with just one bag and lots of crying. Mum brought her back to their house to stay.

He liked Auntie Eunice. She was also a nurse, like his mum, but she looked after old people in a home, while Joey's mum worked shifts in a hospital. They both worked for the same agency, run by a huge woman from Ghana who was really scary. Joey remembers his mum moaning that the nurses were slave labour, and her observation that you only ever make money in this world by exploiting others. Turns out she was right: Billy makes a fortune from using kids as slaves.

At least his mum got paid.

There is no mention of Joey, and no picture of Joey or Candace. They are not looking for Joey and, so far, it seems that Antiques Colin hasn't grassed. But Joey still doesn't like the vase deal, what if the whole thing is a set-up with Colin? He will take nothing for granted.

Candace wakes up. She opens the big, purple curtains in their room and is disappointed that the day is overcast.

She licks her finger and draws the shape of the sun on the glass.

'What's that for?'

Candace shrugs. 'I just made sunshine because there wasn't any,' she says, with an authority and straightforwardness that makes him want to weep. If only it was that simple.

They go down for breakfast, Candace is trying out all of the cereals.

'I'm having a new breakfast adventure every day,' she declares, copying a lady who takes some yoghurt and honey with hers. She's taken to having several plates at breakfast and has become fond of croissants, a thing she'd never had or even heard of until she came to the Premier Inn. While she enjoys her 'breakfast adventure',

Candace: The Gallery Girl

Joey watches everyone and everything, eyes like a hawk, looking for anything untoward.

Candace looks like a boy, or can at least pass for one. Perhaps a slightly too flamboyant boy. That boy that everyone knows is gay, and when he does a big reveal as a teenager, the family hug him and say, 'We know.' It will do, for now. It has to.

After breakfast they return to the room.

'Teeth,' Joey instructs.

When they go out today, his plan is to take all their stuff with them, to leave nothing in the room. The rucksacks are packed and they head out of the door. They have an hour and a half until the auction begins. It's plenty of time, but Joey wants to get to the area early. He wants to get inside, into a crowd, knowing that it will be safer if they are surrounded by people. There will be some level of security there, there'd have to be, with valuable *objets d'art*. Joey will sit near security guards, make sure that they position themselves by the exits.

He double-checks the room. 'Remember, you're Reggie today.'

Candace nods, happy to play the game.

They leave the hotel to head for King's Cross Station. Joey looks left and right, and scans the street and buildings around them. A blue BMW drives past the hotel entrance, the same sort as before. Fuck. He stands outside the station pretending to do up Candace's shoelace. He can look around. They both look so different from how they did before. Joey thinks he looks like a jazz teacher with his trilby, sunglasses and loose white linen shirt, beige Chinos and sandals. Candace just looks like a little boy, a happy, well looked after little boy, out with his dad. He stands up and faces the other way, whilst he pretends to scroll through his phone. Two men who look like the two who were in Tate Modern walk across the road, straight past Joey and Candace toward the station. Joey didn't tell Antiques Colin where they were staying, and there is no way he could have tracked them.

Or is there?

Joey walks up to the taxi rank, his heart pounding.

He takes Candace's hand as he opens the door and they both get in. He looks back to see where the two men are. They are climbing into the blue BMW – the driver has pulled up by the pavement. Billy has people *everywhere*. He must have eyes and ears in all the hotels in London. They won't be going back.

They have time to kill. Joey asks the driver to do a bit of a sightseeing tour, so that 'Reggie' can see some more of London. He gives Candace a big wink as he says this. He points to all the main sights, they even go past Westminster and Buckingham Palace. Joey knows this will be a good way to lose anyone who may have been following them.

Billy is after him, he's sure of that. He wants Candace, he wants the money and he wants Joey. But the brutal reality is that he wants Joey dead.

The knowledge is strangely calming, even though Joey is scared.

Candace is quiet. They've spent so much time together over the last few months that their moods seem to transfer across to each other.

The song 'We're Walking On Sunshine' ends on the driver's radio, and it's on the hour, so they go to a news bulletin. There's international news first, something about Trump, then regional stories. The presenter says, 'Police are still looking for a person of interest, Billy O'Shea, in connection with the murder of a 24-year-old old single mother.'

Joey finds it disturbing how the police and the news hardly ever mention the name County Lines, as if by doing so, they could start a civil war. It's not a 'local' drugs gang, for fuck's sake. They never want to admit that it's bigger than that. That this country is overrun with child exploitation. They've let it get out of control and now they can't stop it. It's been going on for years.

Joey thinks they're going to move on to another story, but then, for the first time in this nightmare, they name Candace. A woman, Catherine-something, who is introduced as having some senior role at children's services, speaks. 'We are extremely concerned for the wellbeing of this little girl, Candace Murphy. She is missing and hasn't been since the attack. Police suspect that she might be a witness, and might have been taken by her mother's assailant.'

It's too late. Candace heard every word. She looks at Joey, eyes as wide open as garage doors. Joey squeezes her hand and leans in. 'Shhh, keep very quiet. Good girl.'

Candace squeezes his hand back. He knows she trusts him, probably more than anyone she ever has.

Joey knows exactly who that woman is: she's the voice he heard on the phone to Billy talking dirty to him when Billy didn't know that he was in the flat. This is the woman that Billy's been connected to for years, since he was a teenager in care himself.

And this woman is making a personal plea to get Candace back. There's only one reason. She wants her back to protect Billy. Perhaps even to give over to Billy. The two of them are in cahoots. They must be. Candace isn't safe wherever she goes.

Joey thinks about what to do next.

His plan was to leave Candace at the auction house; someone would eventually call the police from there. Or to drop her off at the council offices on his way to the airport.

But hearing that woman's voice means that Candace isn't safe, even in the hands of the authorities.

Now he knows that he must protect Candace from more than just Billy.

It changes everything.

XXIX

Joey

They arrive on time for the auction, not early, as Joey had hoped. Their little sightseeing tour plunged them into heavy traffic – and it means that he doesn't get a chance to scope out the area. He's cross with himself, because he doesn't know quite what he's walking into.

Antiques Colin is already there, as welcoming and jolly as he always has been. He is dressed less flamboyantly today than he has been when Joey has been at his home. Today he's wearing a cream linen suit and white shirt, with a red paisley scarf hanging around his neck and some very polished, expensive-looking brogues. He also has a trilby, made of cream straw, and is carrying a large leather messenger bag. He looks every inch the epitome of a debonair antiques dealer, as though he is playing the part in a film.

Maybe too much the part? Joey is suspicious.

Colin raises his hat to Candace and does not comment on the fact that she is dressed as a boy. Joey doesn't know what to make of that either.

Colin waves them in through the door, quickly introducing Joey to the auctioneer, who is sipping a cup of tea and looking over his notes. Colin then takes them over to meet some people in a little room behind a large glass window. They wave hello; Colin obviously has a great deal of influence here.

Colin takes the vase and gives it to a man in the room who prints out a bit of paper. Joey is invited in to sign it, then a copy is made for him and another one for the staff. Everyone seems friendly and relaxed, but Joey is in no danger of letting his guard down. He trusts no one.

Candace stays close, holding Joey's hand tight. Joey hasn't spoken about the news on the radio and Candace hasn't asked. Does she understand what the word 'murder' means?

Back out front in the auction house, the room has filled up. Judging by the different accents and languages, there are a lot of different nationalities here.

Colin directs them to some chairs on the far side near the front. 'Help yourself to the buffet, there are sandwiches and nibbles.'

Joey politely shakes his head, just as a swarm of people dressed in black and grey swoop in and clear the table of the free food.

Colin looks askance and then turns back to Joey. 'Well, perhaps not.'

Colin sits next to Joey, and Candace shuffles across to sit on Joey's lap. She nestles in and puts her hand on his arm.

Joey is watching everyone. He has his eye on the security men and wishes he was closer to the exit, but that part of the room is filled with Chinese and Russians who, apparently, according to Colin, love Satsuma ware.

The auction begins.

Candace thinks it's funny how fast the man speaks. 'He's not talking properly,' she whispers.

'He's in a hurry, because there are lots of things for sale to get through,' Joey explains. He catches himself sounding like a teacher. Or maybe a father. He has to stop those thoughts.

Colin wriggles in his chair and then gives Joey a nudge. 'Lot 7, that's you.'

Colin is holding a basic printed brochure with some information about each item in the sale and black and white pictures, with a promise that more detail is available online.

The auctioneer's assistant is wearing white gloves as he holds up the vase for the buyers to see.

'This is a recent addition to auction,' the auctioneer begins. 'It was only added two days ago. A rare Satsuma porcelain bowl, crafted by Yabu Meizan. An early piece, dated from before 1800.'

The assistant turns it round under the light, pointing to the markings.

The auctioneer starts the bidding at £5,000.

Joey frowns. That seems a little low. He was hoping he could get over £10k from the sale and then get out of here. But, as Joey watches, arms start to wave in the air all over the room. As the hands go up, so does the price. There are eight people on a counter taking telephone bids. Joey hasn't seen the vase on the website, but it must be good, especially as the only pictures available were the snapshots he sent over when he photographed the vase in the Italian restaurant on the South Bank.

Within a matter of seconds, the bidding has reached 15k and is still going up. Joey is excited but remains hyper-vigilant, trying not to be distracted by this good fortune. Are things finally going to start to go his way? He holds Candace tight while continuing to scan the room, or at least, everywhere that's in his range. He can't look behind him, but if Billy wants him dead and has sent someone to do the deed, then they'll wait until he has the money, no question. As Joey keeps reminding himself, Billy is addicted to money.

The auction keeps going. The auctioneer talks so quickly it's hard to take it all in. Colin sits next to Joey, smiling away, alternating between looking at Joey, then looking back to the room. It keeps going up and up. The bidding reaches 30k. Joey can't believe it. This can't be real. He is feeling shocked. Up it still goes in 5k increments. Another 5k, another 5k. Who are these people with money to burn on an old pot that doesn't even look that great. Joey starts to feel overwhelmed. It reaches 70k. Then, at 80k, the auctioneer raises his hammer. 'Going once, going twice—' Before the hammer falls, another bid comes in via the phone.

Candace: The Gallery Girl

'And at 90k, sold!'

Joey looks at Colin in shock, barely able to believe what's just happened. Colin pumps his hand up and down and slaps him on the back. Colin also congratulates Candace.

He stands. 'You'll be wanting your money. Follow me.'

They head off back to the little room behind. Joey is told that it normally takes 30 days to receive the money. His heart sinks. He'd hoped to just pocket the cash and get out.

'But on this occasion,' the member of staff explains, 'Colin has covered the waiting time and you will receive the money as soon as the American bidder's money goes through.' They all seem to know each other backstage, and this is how they do business.

'How long will that be?' Joey asks.

'It should happen fairly quickly…' the man says, with a nod and a smile. Joe rings for a cab to pick them up, and it isn't long before Joey is given a large brown envelope of cash. He looks inside and thinks, 'Yeah, that looks about right.'

He shakes Colin's hand once more and explains that they have to go. 'My taxi is outside.'

Colin looks around him as if trying to make a decision. 'Hang on, I'll walk out with you.'

They stand outside the taxi. Colin says, 'I never liked Billy, you know. He's a scourge on humanity. He'll be after you and Candace.'

He passes Joey a piece of paper.

'Here's the number of a dear friend of mine who used to work for the government. He has set up his own little enterprise manufacturing passports. They will cost approximately £10,000 each. But you can afford that now.' Colin smiles.

Joey hands over the 2k of coke as promised.

Colin says, 'I'm very grateful. And, not that it will matter to you, but this is my last party. I'm moving to France. I have a little house there. It's time. I must confess, I don't like what County Lines is doing to this country. There used to be honour and cooperation amongst thieves, as it were, but not now. Not anymore. Now we have too many migrant criminals. Don't get me wrong, good migrants are fine; they keep us going, but who is letting in the gangs? And why? That's the big question, and that's why my good friend left his government role and now helps people leave this country.' He looks at Joey sadly. 'I'm afraid I'm done with it all. I'm ready to live a much quieter life, get away from London and run my little brocante. I set it up years ago with Larry, before he died. I just want out now.'

Joey knows how he feels.

'So, I wish you well. Have a good onward journey, and look after little Candace, the poor mite.'

As Joey shakes his hand again, Colin says, 'My surname is Adams. Do look me up if you are in the Cognac area.'

'Bye, Mr Antiques. Give my love to Cotton,' Candace says as Joey and Candace get in the taxi and head to Victoria Station.

For the first time, Joey dares to believe that now, with this huge amount of money behind him, he might really, truly, make his way out of this. Is it possible that the antiques world is one place that Billy doesn't have eyes and ears in?

And, once again, it's been a little bit too easy. Here's someone handing him a ridiculous amount of money and an escape route with passports.

Surely Billy, with his bloody *Antiques Roadshow* obsession, could have recognised that vase if he had looked properly. He'd always said it was valuable. Maybe, given all the chaos, he doesn't even know it's missing.

Or, carrying more cash than he's ever dreamt of, is Joey still a dead man walking?

He feels exhausted, wired by the state of heightened alert his body has been in for days. But he hears those words again in his head, 'This is so easy.'

Is it? Could it be?

XXX

Joey

Candace sits tight, right up next to Joey on the seat of the taxi.

'Am I still Reggie?' she asks.

'For now. Is that okay?'

She nods, satisfied. He knows that she will soon be asking questions, about her mum, about Billy, about her life. She doesn't have anyone else. He needs to keep her safe. He needs to keep both of them safe.

At Victoria Station, Candace asks when the next train will be coming.

'I don't know,' he says, truthfully, because he doesn't know where they're going. He has some decisions to make, and he isn't ready.

'Can I do some colouring. Or some drawing?' she asks.

Joey smiles. 'Yeah, sure. Why not?'

They go into WHSmith and she walks toward the arts and crafts section. She pulls out a packet of felt tip pens and a sketchbook.

'Anything else?'

She shakes her head. 'No, I just want to do some drawing.'

He knows how that feels. It makes Joey feel warm inside as he remembers how much he loved drawing and making things. He buys himself a small sketchbook and some fine point black pens.

'Snap,' Joey says.

'I've got more colours than you.'

'Can't we share?'

Candace thinks for a moment. 'Yeah, 'spose.'

They walk to the food hall and spend some time deciding what they want to eat.

Candace spots a Burger King and smiles. Joey fancied something Mexican, but is more than happy to let Candace have what she wants. He cares about her more than he had let himself realise. He feels proud that she is drawing and has talents. He wants her to go to school, he wants her to flourish, he just needs to get as far away from here as possible to enable that to happen.

Perhaps this is the point of being alive, Joey thinks. To feel fleeting moments like this. Sometimes just seconds of peace. And love.

They sit on the benches by the train times screen and eat their burgers. Next to Joey is a copy of *the Metro*, the free paper, that someone has left on the seat. He opens it up and lights on an article about the new Tate gallery, the Turner Contemporary in Margate on the Kent coast in honour of Tracey Emin.

Her name is familiar to him, vaguely. An artist. He'd heard of her when he was at school. *The Metro* article about Tracey Emin highlights the new gallery's impact on the town's regeneration, and celebrates Emin's personal connection to Margate, the town where she grew up. Joey's never been to that part of the world, but it has inspired a contemporary artist and that makes it interesting to him. Maybe he could even be persuaded to like Turner. The article talks about some of Emin's more recent artistic endeavours. It mentions her support for the local community, and her plans for an art school.

The article also touches on the gallery's role in showcasing Turner's work and its contribution to the town's cultural landscape. He learns that Emin has exhibited her work there, including her famous piece 'My Bed' and has participated in events there. She's even projected a poem, her 'love letter to Turner', onto the building's facade.

Joey is totally absorbed in this article and suddenly realises that he's been distracted, looking at his phone, looking at the newspaper. He hasn't been keeping up his usual lookout. He scans the concourse. His eyes alight on one particular board, the 15:53 from Victoria to Margate. It takes just under two hours to get there.

It would be good to get a couple of hours away from London tonight. Perhaps it's time that Candace learned to appreciate some landscapes!

The train leaves in 45 minutes. Why not?

He looks around, sucks in his cheeks and says to Candace. 'Righto. Let's go and get our tickets.'

She obediently puts her drawing materials in her rucksack. Joey has not taken his own rucksack off since they left the auction house, and will not until they are somewhere safe tonight. They push open the heavy glass doors into the ticket and information office and Joey buys two tickets to Margate.

'Is Margate by the sea?' Candace asks.

'Yep.'

'Is there a Sealife Centre?'

'Nope. But they've got something better.'

'What?'

'Tell you when we get there.' He sticks his tongue out at her.

She raises her eyes to heaven, as though she is the adult and he is the child, being silly. He loves goofing around with her.

Tickets bought, they move to a different seating area. Candace is tired now, but not too tired to notice a little sweet shop.

'D'ya think they have ice creams there?'

Having let his guard down for a moment, Joey is twitchy once more, looking all over the station like a meerkat, unable to keep his head still. They walk over. There is a freezer inside the shop. Candace seems to take an age choosing her ice-lolly. She finally settles on a Fab.

'Because I'm fab,' she says.

And it's true, Joey thinks. She's a terrific kid. But he's not going to tell her that. He catches himself feeling like a dad again, proud of his daughter. He feels so much relief that his plan has changed. There is no way he could have left Candace to those people. She would disappear without a trace into a murky underworld of abuse. She deserves so much more than that.

He pays and off they go again. Keep moving, keep moving. He picks up a couple of bottles of water and waits to see which platform the train to Margate will be. He keeps looking around, touching his rucksack. He's got to calm down or he'll draw attention to himself just by how on edge he is.

Candace stands in front of him, and he finds himself holding onto the straps of her rucksack. His finger unconsciously strokes her shoulder to keep her comforted. As soon as the platform number comes up, people start flooding along the station. He holds her hand and notices that the bottom of the ice lolly is dripping onto her hand, because she's eating it too slowly. As they walk past a coffee stall, he grabs some paper serviettes from the counter so he can wipe the mess away. Thinking like a parent again. He laughs at himself and shakes his head.

They get on the train. Joey is back on heightened alert, satisfied that they haven't been followed. They find a seat with a table and she sits next to him, taking the window seat. He puts her bag above them on the rack, but places his rucksack on the floor and threads his foot in and out of the straps, so the bag can't leave him without him knowing.

Their bottles of water are on the table. Candace finishes the last bit of her lolly and her hands are sticky. He tips some water onto the serviette and wipes her perfect, little brown hands. He smiles.

'You okay, Reggie?'

She nods.

He wipes around her sticky mouth.

She sets to with the drawing and Joey begins to look out of the window.

He drinks his water down quickly, he can feel a headache coming on. He hasn't got any paracetamol, so he hopes that rehydrating will do the trick. He looks at the names of the stations, rolling them around his tongue: Chatham, Whitstable, Herne Bay. With each mile that the train rolls away from London, he feels happier. Though he knows they'll have to go a lot further than the south coast to escape Billy.

When they get out at Margate, they walk out the front of the station and spot a Premier Inn close by.

It faces the sea.

They book themselves in. The room is bigger than the King's Cross one, which meets with Candace's approval. Joey laughs at the fact that he's got 100k to his name and he's still booking himself into a Premier Inn.

They sit on the beach with more ice creams, proper ones this time, with flakes, enjoying the evening sunshine. Joey pulls out the phone number that Colin gave him. He realises that this is the next step. They both need passports, and then they'll be gone. He'll do it. He'll do it tonight.

They get fish 'n' chips for tea. Candace is tired, rubbing her eyes. It's been another big day. Tonight they can rest.

'Tomorrow we'll look round Margate and visit the Turner Gallery,' Joey tells her. A little holiday before the next stage of their life.

'I don't like Turner,' she says.

'You might. People change.'

XXXI

Joey

When Candace is asleep, Joey calls the number Colin gave him and outlines what he needs.

The man on the other end is factual and business-like and has been expecting his call.

'For various reasons, it's unlikely that Candace has an existing passport,' Joey explains.

'All to the good. If she doesn't, it will be easier,' the man says.

The passport man suggests that they find new names that are close in sound to their old ones.

Joey hasn't thought about a new name. What can you do with 'Samaroo' that sounds similar. He's busy thinking when the passport man, who, for all his talk about names, is choosing to remain anonymous, says something that Joey knows is one of those sliding doors moments in his life.

'Will the girl now be your daughter?'

There's a moment's pause.

'She will,' he says. It feels like saying, 'I do.'

In the morning, Joey takes Candace to the Photo-Me booth just outside the station. He clocked it yesterday when they first arrived. Joey has to get four photos of each of them to the passport man, who runs his operation from his home, so to keep things secure he will only meet Joey in a public café.

Joey has been thinking about new names. He can't seem to do anything with Samaroo. For some reason, he remembers that his mum had friends back in Trinidad who she spoke about a lot. They sent each other Christmas and birthday cards. She'd call them up once a month or so, because it was expensive. Her mum's friend's name was Naomi Baptiste. She was a good friend, and he remembers his mum always laughing with her on the phone. Baptiste will be their surname. He likes it. It also makes him think about being baptised. Not in a religious kind of a way, but as in beginning a new life. A fresh start. Cleansed and purified.

He thinks about a new first name. Another version of Joseph could work – maybe 'Giuseppe'? No, he doesn't look Italian. Maybe 'Youssef'? He likes it, but it's Arabic and people are racist about Arabs. The stereotype is that they are the bad people. He laughs inside and thinks of his time back in prison when he learnt quickly that all people could be bad. The Albanians were always dubbed the scariest, but Joey's not so sure, because Irish Billy Bananas is very scary indeed.

Joey tries not to think about Billy.

Candace: The Gallery Girl

He knows Billy will still be out looking for him. He knows Billy will want him dead. He knows Billy will never stop looking. Will he always have to look over his shoulder to check that Billy isn't there?

He also knows that Billy wants Candace, because he wants to sell her. Selling a child. It would be horrific if this was hundreds of years ago, but this is the 21st century. As he thinks this, he looks at Candace's kind face as she stares into the camera. He makes a promise to himself that he'll never let anything bad happen to her.

He settles on Józef as a name. It's Dutch, which has a nice cosmopolitan feel, and he likes the way the letters shape on the page. Yes, he likes the sound of Józef Baptiste.

He tries to get Candace to sit still so they can take the necessary photo, but she keeps fidgeting and making faces. He laughs with her. She seems so relaxed and normal, not the grieving child of a murdered mother. Candace is behaving like a normal girl her age, and he's pleased about that. He realises with a bit of a shock that he still doesn't actually know her age, or when her birthday is.

After 16 photos of Candace and another eight of the two of them laughing and pulling faces together, Joey puts the photos in his manbag. They walk back towards the beach to find some breakfast. While they are enjoying their fry-up, Joey asks the café cashier where the Turner is.

'Straight up there, you can't miss it.'

Joey pays and the two walk hand-in-hand toward the Turner Gallery.

The sun shines on their faces and still feels warm, even though summer is nearly over. Joey knows that they have a lot to talk about. They are now going to be bonded together via passports. In the eyes of the law, he'll be her father. The eyes of the law have never mattered much to him in the past, but he realises that they do now. He works out that he would have been in his early 20s when she was born, which is perfectly feasible.

They walk toward the Turner building, taking their time, enjoying the morning, enjoying being away from London and without a timetable of drops to do. They stop and lean over the rail by the harbour. Candace has never seen boats like this before, not in real life. He points out different ones: a blue and white stripey boat, a yellow boat, one with a very tall mast. She chooses which one she likes the most.

'That one!'

There is a little boat with a white top and orange underside. On the side is painted the name *Kassandra*. Joey looks at the name for a bit and tries to think why it rings a bell. He thinks 'Kassandra' might have been a character in *Only Fools and Horses,* a sitcom his mum used to enjoy. He smiles and then dredges up a distant memory from school about Kassandra being Greek and known for something – but he can't remember what. He remembers the primary school teacher, Mrs Turner – God, was that really her name? Like the artist – and remembers how much he liked school when he was young, before he was kidnapped by County Lines, before they stole him from his life.

When he feels the wetness of tears gathering in the corner of his eyes, he tries to pull himself together, tells himself to stop being so soft. But he realises that the tears aren't for him, they are bitterness about just how *big* and unstoppable the County Lines system is.

He turns his head towards Candace, this precious bundle of energy and imagination and life, who is not going to be taken by them. He picks her up and holds her.

He whispers, so quietly that she can't hear, because the words are for him, 'They're not having you.'

Before they turn to continue their walk to the Gallery, he turns the name 'Kassandra Baptise' around in his head. Yes, he decides. That will be her new name.

'Come on, Cass, let's go.'

'Cass?' Candace queries. 'Is that like Reggie? Are we playing another game?'

'Not a game, this time,' he says, with a determined smile.

There is an installation at the gallery, by a young artist. It's a mixture of painting, drawing, papier-mâché and collage, with bits of fabric in places. There are figures and a boat and Candace is captivated, making up stories about who they are and where they are going.

The information board, which of course Candace can't read, explains that the work explores themes about colonialism and migration, as well as the centrality of the sea in shaping histories of migration and conflict. It seems apt.

When Joey and Candace sit down for lunch in the café, Joey texts the passport man.

I have the photos as requested. New names: Kassandra Baptiste aged six, born 4th July 2019.

He plucks the date because Lorna didn't seem to know, Candace has no idea, and American Independence Day seems good enough.

And Józef Baptiste 1st June 1997.

He just likes the idea of them both having summer birthdays. His real birthday is in January, and he never really liked that time of year. Having new passports really is the new beginning of a new life.

The passport man soon messages back with an Italian café location in St John's Wood. Joey has paid cash for the week in Margate.

So, in two more days, they will travel to London with their passport photos and 25k in cash. The other document Joey has is Lorna's hairdressing certificate, rolled up in his bag. He must have known at some level that Lorna wasn't going to make it out of that flat alive.

The passport man has quoted 20k as his fee, but Joey is well-used to being in debt bondage to Billy, so he thinks it prudent to travel with more, so that he's equipped when the goalposts change, which they surely will.

The next day they continue their 'holiday' with a visit to Dreamland, a seafront amusement park. Candace is in her element, wanting to try every ride. She's never had candyfloss before. Joey's glad her hair is still contained beneath the cap in her boyish, 'Reggie' look, otherwise there could be a lot of sticky mess to sort out later.

He watches everything carefully, still alert, still convinced that Billy, or one of his minions, will appear around any corner.

Instead, he sees the potential exploitation of children at every turn. Seaside places like this attract the type of people he instantly recognises – those who waft around, waiting to prey on the young. Regular visitors are clueless. But he has had so much time to think in these last few days, but also while in prison. It's clear to him just how normal child exploitation is now. In every town, in every attraction and institution built for kids. That parents, families, schools and professionals are still so misinformed, and so, as a society, it has become normalised. Labels and sayings: they're 'just a bad kid', or they've 'gone off the rails', or it's 'just a phase'. Gang bosses are so clever and they have got right into the centre of people's ignorance, laziness and arrogance. They dance around people's lives with glee, while they kidnap their children, take them away from any possibility of a future. He understands how each stolen child is a perverse kind of joy for the gang, another life taken to exploit.

They sell the drugs for profit, but there are many others who come along for the ride. The sickos who want to molest children – like whoever was in the deal to 'buy' Candace. The drugs have blurred the moral lines. Like Colin Adams, interior designer and antiques dealer, friend and ally in their escape. He, like so many Joey has met, is alright, on one level. He's helped them – more than he needed to. He's put himself out. But at the same time, he's not alright. He's in a world where he's supplying drugs to his clients and associating with people who hold abhorrent views about children. Joey knows he's becoming cynical, but it's the reality he's experienced.

Drugs always make people twisted.

XXXII

Joey

In spite of the early night that Joey has insisted on because they have to be at St John's Wood by 10am, Candace struggles to wake up when the alarm goes off. Joey realises that he isn't leaping out of bed either. They are both beginning to relax. It's good on one level — that holiday vibe is kicking in good and proper — but it's also risky. They can't be off their guard. He can't, at least.

Candace, or Cass as she is now being called by Joey, is also showing a seriously cheeky side that he hasn't fully seen before. The girl has sass! Perhaps she kept it hidden because of Billy. She's smart as well as funny.

They get to the station with very little time to spare to catch the train to London, and get across town via the underground. Cass is still dressed as a boy, and no rucksack this time, that is back in the hotel. Joey carries his rucksack with him, even to the toilet. It does not come off, apart from when he sleeps, and even then it's in the bed with him.

Joey is dressed in his trilby and shades once more,

and he's wearing sandals again. No one from his tribe would dream of dressing like this, in chinos and linen. He wonders if it will always feel like playing a part. Or perhaps it was the old him that was acting. Who knows?

They get to the Italian café by the appointed time. The instructions were to sit outside and put the little plant table decoration, that should sit in the middle of the table, onto a spare chair nearest the door of the café.

A man comes over and invites them in to sit at a table. He orders coffee for him and Joey and asks Candace what she would like.

'A chocolate milkshake, please.'

Joey gives her a pen and she starts drawing on the napkins, absorbed in her work as the men lean into each other and start talking in earnest.

'Once I have the photos, I'll meet you back here in two hours with the finished product.'

It's just like the drug world, where people find language to avoid saying what they really mean. 'Finished product' is a fine euphemism for the documents that are going to change their lives. He confirms that the price is 20k in cash in an envelope.

Joey agrees and is relieved that the price hasn't changed. He hates the shifting sands of County Lines, where you never really know quite how much you are in for and they gaslight the hell out of children and their families. Perhaps the world of hooky passports is less like the County Lines underworld.

Candace: The Gallery Girl

They wander around the shops while they wait for the passport man to complete his work and return. Joey has a sudden shudder of fear. *What if this is all a set-up?* What if Billy is here, lurking in the shadows, waiting to pounce just at the moment Joey thinks he can get away. Toying with him. Still intent on his deal to take Candace and sell her to some one as a sex toy. She's six, for God's sake. Six years old. Joey is beginning to get himself worked up all over again. He knows – mostly through Billy – how fucked up some people are. Why this should also equate to the ones who have money, big money, he doesn't know. But Joey has seen how money makes people mad and crazy, fucks them up until they think they are better than everyone, like gods who can choose other people's destiny. It's sick.

Just as when they were in the amusement park, Joey notices much more these days, about what's going on around him. He notes how wealthy the area is and how that passport man, who looks like a university lecturer, must be making a fortune.

They pass the time wandering the streets, Joey watching and looking the whole time. Two hours is up. They walk toward the café and the man is already there, sitting down. He calls the waitress over and smiles. He clearly likes his job. He hands Joey two blue passports. He opens them discreetly on his lap and can't believe that they are fake. They look exactly like the real thing.

Joey says, 'They're good.' He pauses. 'What did you do in the civil service?'

He smiles. 'IT.'

That could mean anything, Joey reflects. He hands over the envelope in payment. He has already taken out the additional 5k.

The man smiles again. 'I hope you have a pleasant onward journey.'

Almost the same words that Colin used when he wished them well. Joey fervently hopes they do. They stand up to depart, Joey watching everyone and everywhere, eyes in the back of his head.

He feels nervous. He doesn't want to be on public transport, so calls a cab. He and Candace get in and head to Victoria Station. It's only four miles, but four miles across the capital can take an age. At the station he goes to the ticket window and buys the Margate bound ticket with cash. Safely on the train, they both look out of the window, fields and trees all zooming by like a fast-forwarding video of his life.

From out of nowhere, Candace suddenly asks, 'Is my mummy dead?'

Joey has a lump in his throat, but he holds her little hand and squeezes it. He's not going to lie. 'Yes,' he says, solemnly. 'Your mummy has gone to heaven.'

She leans into Joey and sucks her thumb. Joey looks at the seat across from him, where a kid is seated. A nervous kid in a dark hoodie, with a black rucksack, keeps checking his phone.

There's also an elder two seats in front, facing the kid,

keeping an eye. Joey knows this set-up. Too well. The kid won't have a ticket. County Lines doesn't fund travel costs. Joey watches. The kid's eyes dart everywhere, he wipes his hands down his black tracksuit bottoms where his palms are sweating. Joey sees a version of his younger self, scared to death, out of his depth, about to take a leap into the abyss. But what can he do? The reach is too big.

Joey sees a notice on the glass partition next to the suitcase hold.

See it, say it, sort it.

It's information from the transport police and a number where you can send texts if you see something suspicious.

Joey looks away, back out of the window. It's not his business. The kid is not his problem.

Then looks back and plumbs the number into his phone. Why not? He calls it in. He will help this child, because that's what this kid is, a child. He will help him, like he wishes someone had helped him, if they had known what they were looking at.

It works.

At Ramsgate, the transport police are suddenly in the carriage. They approach the child and take him out onto the station, where there are other police waiting on the platform.

The elder sits with his hood up, frantically texting.

But a hand lands on his shoulder, too, and takes the elder outside, handcuffed, to be with some different police who have a van ready for him. The younger boy is taken to a police car on the other side of the road. He is not handcuffed and he's crying.

The kid wouldn't thank him now if he'd known what Joey has done, but perhaps he might, one day into the future.

It's enough.

A tannoy announcement apologises for the delay, and promises that they will be on their way in just a moment.

Joey's phone vibrates in his hand.

He looks at his phone. There's a text message.

Mr Bananas is looking for you. Be careful, lose the phone.

Fuck.

It's from Colin Adams.

Joey feels scared. He doesn't know what to do. Fuck.

Joey leaps up, pulling a bewildered Candace with him. They leave the train at Ramsgate and cross the platform for trains to Dover. Joey puts his phone in the bin on the Ramsgate platform.

'Aren't we going back to the hotel?'

Joey shakes his head.

'Are we still on holiday?'

Joey's had better holidays, but he nods.

When they get to Dover they buy some snacks and a few bottles of water. Joey is beyond stressed but tries so hard not to show it. Candace is now enjoying being called Cassy.

'I like it,' she says. 'I never really liked Candy anyway. It sounds babyish.' She pauses for a moment. 'Am I a grown up now I don't have a mum?'

Candace: The Gallery Girl

'Oh, Cass.'

They head quickly towards the ferry.

'I don't have my rucksack.'

'I'll get you a new one.'

They only have a few items, but lots of money. And that's all they need.

Joey's eyes are everywhere. There are men in roadman clothes, black hoodies, puffer jackets, it's a uniform. Fuck.

He stands in line as a foot passenger and holds out both passports. He is sweating, he has never been so nervous. The man at passport control looks at them, studies them like he's going to write a fucking dissertation on the pair of them. Candace is still dressed like a boy. The passport control man is so slow to do anything, Joey thinks he might explode.

He frowns, leans down towards Candace and says, 'What's your name, then?'

Joey thinks he's going to be sick. He will be arrested and end up back in prison and Billy will destroy him. He will be dead. Candace will be dead.

But Candace shows her teeth to the passport control man, presenting him with her brightest and best smile.

'Cassy,' she says, very firmly.

The passport control man peers at her and then at Joey, who does a very small smile, the corners of his mouth twitching upwards almost out of his control.

'We're on holiday!' Candace tells him.

'Lucky you,' the man says.

'And I've never been on a boat before,' she declares.

Then the man nods and lets them through. 'Enjoy your trip.'

Joey has momentarily forgotten to breathe. But he pulls himself together and, as they get on the ferry, he strides with purpose, holding Cassy's hand.

The crossing is only an hour and a half, but it's past lunchtime and they order food. Cassy is happy eating her lunch, oblivious to the paralysing fear that has gripped Joey.

Joey watches the TV screen mindlessly. He is utterly exhausted, but he can't believe that he is on the ferry leaving England.

Die, or leave the country.

He feels overwhelmed by the enormity of it all.

The news comes on the screen.

A man was found dead at his home in Ladbroke Grove early this morning.

Joey sits up.

Colin Adams was a successful interior designer to the stars. Police have made a connection between this murder and the recent murder of Lorna Murphy, who was found dead in her flat nearly two weeks ago. Police are looking for this man, Billy O'Shea, in connection with both attacks.

The next part of the bulletin gives a description of Billy and further warnings about not approaching him given the danger he may present to the public. The numbers are given out for how to report any sighting.

Cassy looks up, just as Billy's face disappears from the screen.

Joey rubs his chin and swallows. He can smell his hands, the sweat, fear and panic on them. But Cassy doesn't seem to notice. She looks relaxed. Fine. Just a six-year-old girl on her first boat trip.

At Calais, Joey changes several hundred pounds' worth of cash into Euros.

They are on foreign soil. Die, or leave the country. Is it enough?

They head to the shops to buy clothes for Cassy. There are shops at the Calais Coeur De Vie. Cassy can choose whatever she wants.

'Girls' clothes?'

'Yep. And a new rucksack. A big one.'

They also buy pyjamas, socks, knickers, new trainers and some toiletries.

Joey buys himself another whole new outfit, so that he has a spare one in his own rucksack. He quite likes this new vibe now, no longer the roadman. Instead, he looks like he could be a presenter from *Top Gear* with his loose, floral, cotton shirt. They buy more art supplies, too. Cassy asks for a mobile phone.

Joey says, 'No,' without a moment's hesitation.

Cassy pouts for a moment, but then Joey is kinder. 'You're too young. Maybe when you're a bit bigger.' God, how do you ever protect them from what's out there? What a responsibility.

After stopping for cake and coffee, and a 'real croissant in French France,' they head to the train station once more.

Calais is too close to London. France is too close to England.

On the train, Cassy sits next to Joey and pulls his arms around her.

'Are *you* my daddy?'

Joey holds back the tears that threaten to come again. He strokes her head to give him more time to compose his vocal chords into something that might not crack with emotion.

'Yes, Cassy, it looks like I am.'

She snuggles in further to him. 'Yay,' she says, then falls asleep, almost instantly. He feels a warm sense of something he hasn't felt for a long time, certainly not as an adult. Perhaps it's love.

The journey takes more than four hours. Cassy sleeps for most of it. Joey can't bring himself to. Not yet. As before, the black rucksack is woven around his feet so no one can take it.

They pull into their destination. The concourse is very grand, with a marble-looking floor and grey pillars going up to the ceiling.

'It's like a gallery,' Cassy says, looking up at the art nouveau frescoes and ceilings in the station.

When they step outside, it's the very blue light of almost dark.

Joey flags a taxi and shows the driver an address that is written on a loose piece of paper. They sit in the back and see the world outside their window disappear into the darkness of night. Cassy doesn't ask where they are going. She has become used to heading somewhere new, trusting Joey to take care of her.

They pull up outside a new-looking townhouse. Joey pays the driver. He's never been here before, but this must be it. Cassy sleepily follows Joey to a front door. He rings the doorbell and steps back. He hears a bolt going back, and a lady answers the door with a frown.

'Joey?' she peers at him.

'Auntie?'

The woman screeches and then calls out, 'It's Joey! It's Joey! Joey's here!'

Joey's mum walks to the door, her eyes wide in disbelief. Then she is running towards him, arms open to throw them around him.

'Joey!'

She notices who he has with him.

'And who's this?'

The explanations can come later.

'Mummy, this is my girl. Kassandra.'

Afterword

According to the National Police Chiefs' Council, a woman is killed by a man every three days in the UK. Every three days! Violence against women and girls makes up just under 20% of all recorded crime in England and Wales. In the year ending March 2023, police recorded more than 100,000 rape and serious sexual offences. Sadly, because of the current levels of economic and social dysfunction within our society, there are too many Lornas.

Candace, in real-life, is actually an amalgamation of several different children I have worked with who were trapped by County Lines before they were seven years old. I have fictionalised elements of their stories in order to protect them.

The real-life individuals on whom Billy and Ricky are based, were in competition with each other as heads of rival gangs. But neither of them realised that if they went just a little higher up the chain, they actually shared the same bosses. That's deliberate, in the power hierarchy. The modus operandi from the leaders in County Lines is to keep the gangs full of hate, stir things up and keep them active rivals. It's good for business because it stops them becoming lazy or complacent. It also keeps the media busy and the public fear going with stories of stabbings and shootings. Headlines that distract from the real story.

Fear is power.

People know now that County Lines recruiters are skilled in coercion and grooming.

In fact, what makes them skilled is simply doing loudly, theatrically and for far longer, what most of us do to a greater or lesser extent, in life. Compliments. Gifts. Expensive treats. Flattery.

When two people meet and there is a little chemistry, the flirting begins. Poor Lorna. She never had a chance. Because County Lines do a nice line in fake romance. They are actors and, because of the fact they are not emotionally involved with their subjects, they can go further and can begin to enjoy the hunt before bringing down their prey. They talk about it with each other. They share ideas and tips. This happens on car journeys, inside trap houses and, most of all, in prison. Perhaps they should rename prisons 'crime education centres' or 'academies' of crime with a 24/7 curriculum in criminal dexterity.

For the sake of the story and for the pursuit of hope, Joey's better qualities are exaggerated. That, too, is deliberate – in an attempt to reach young people and hold out a hand of hope to know that, with support, they *can* get away from County Lines.

They don't all need a valuable piece of art, or thousands of pounds to escape. But the real-life Joeys, who renounce their gang lives and devote their time to helping others, do have to leave their areas for good. They have to get their tattoos removed. They live in perpetual fear, always looking over their shoulders.

It's not atonement, because often, as in Joey's case, they have done very little wrong and are victims themselves. They don't get a happy ending because their mental health is in pieces. They have had their childhood stolen from them. And yet they carry on. Their desire is to stop other young people going into gangs and to get them out of gangs. It is gallant, important work which often goes unrecognised.

I think that's heroic.

Part of the purpose in telling this tale is to celebrate that heroism.

If you are concerned about a child or young person, help is out there.

Acknowledgements

To my wonderful family, for all their understanding and encouragement. I try very hard not to worry them, but that isn't always easy.

To the team at Mirror Books who work so carefully and with such enthusiasm. They have a beady eye to make sure all is well, and manage to do that with kindness. Particular thanks to Jo Sollis, my editor, who is supportive and wise.

Thank you, as always, to my writing companion, Theresa Gooda, who, like me, has passion and energy in abundance, but thankfully, sometimes a little more sense.

Many thanks to Jane Graham Maw, my very special agent, who checks and double checks and then checks again.

As ever, thank you also to Catherine Lloyd, Alex Plowman and Karen Furse. They always have first eyes on the manuscript and each brings unique insight and guidance. They are so valued, and always such fun to work with.

I'm grateful to a very special woman who I can't name, but who said to me, 'Sometimes good people have to do bad things.' You know who you are.

Of course, I wouldn't be able to tell these stories without the help of my close contacts in this sector, who live and operate in the shadows because they have to. Thank you for everything that you do.

I write these books for the girls and women who endure not only the abuse and exploitation and resulting tragedy, but who also have to put up with society's judgements along the way. It's not their fault. They are not to blame and it isn't fair or accurate to be critical. It's definitely not helpful.

My heart also goes out to the families, growing in number, who have been and are impacted by this huge, dark operation of County Lines.

And finally, a plea to the perpetrators: leave our children alone.

Help and Information

I am the founder of Spark Sisterhood. The traditional goodbye-and-good-luck approach for girls leaving care is outdated. It leaves girls vulnerable to cycles of struggle and adversity, incl. social exclusion, homelessness, unemployment, drug abuse and other challenges. We're here to change that narrative. With our employment pathways, mentoring program, community and online learning platform, we're reshaping post-care experiences for girls across the UK.

Website: https://www.sparksisterhood.org
Email: louise@louise-allen.com

Escapeline is a charity committed to the prevention of the criminal and sexual exploitation of young people by gangs across South West England. For years, thousands of children have been exploited through the practice of County Lines, in which highly organised urban gangs take over provincial drugs markets. County Line gangs are increasing their operations to recruit local youngsters from small towns rather than the big cities and South West England has been particularly targeted.

Escapeline help young people to stay safe by educating them about how child exploitation and grooming works in their local area and teaching them protective strategies.

Website: https://www.escapeline.org.uk
Phone: 0800 389 3899
Email: enquiries@escapeline.org.uk

SLAVE GIRLS
OTHER BOOKS IN THE SERIES

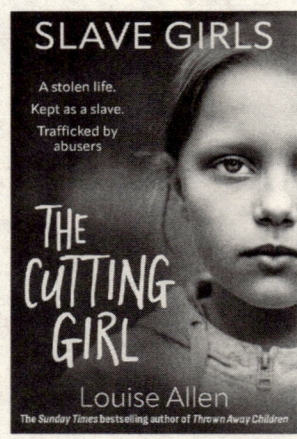

The Cutting Girl
Louise Allen
with Theresa McEvoy

Charlotte - The Cutting Girl - comes from a family of high achievers. Her father is a politician, and her mother is a senior medical officer.

When she moves from her prestigious boarding school she is groomed by a girl two years her senior, spiralling into a cycle of drugs, self-harm and sexual abuse.

When she goes missing, five other girls do, too. A nationwide media campaign sets out to track them down, but can Charlotte ever escape the gang behind the abduction and abuse?

SLAVE GIRLS
OTHER BOOKS IN THE SERIES

The Shrinking Girl
Louise Allen
with Theresa McEvoy

Hanna - The Shrinking Girl - has always struggled to fit in. The eldest of five kids, her homelife is complicated and poor, and her single mum, Eva, can barely keep their heads above water.

Bullied at school for her obvious signs of poverty, she is happy and relieved when a cool girl makes a move to be her new friend. But this friendship carries a terrible cost. She is thrown into a dark world of drugs, gangs, sex and a controlling 'boyfriend'.

Totally controlled by a gang that uses her as a commodity, is there any way she can be pulled from their grip and reunited with her family?